Questions & Answers on the Path of Ascension and Self-Realization

Questions & Answers on the Path of Ascension and Self-Realization

Dr Joshua David Stone

Writers Club Press

San Jose New York Lincoln Shanghai

Questions & Answers on the Path of
Ascension and Self-Realization

Writers Club Press
an imprint of iUniverse.com, Inc.

For information address:
iUniverse.com, Inc.
5220 S 16th, Ste. 200
Lincoln, NE 68512
www.iuniverse.com

ISBN: 0-595-20262-4

Printed in the United States of America

Contents

1

"I took the Decision for Abortion and now I am Suicidal"

Dear Dr. Stone:

I am 25 years of age and married. I am in absolute distress. I used to be spiritual until one incident that rocked my life. I am from a good family, but my parents in haste married me off, although I was not mentally prepared. On top of that, my wife immediately conceived and I was in a total confusion as I was not at all career-wise prepared in this modern world. Even though aware, I took a horrible decision of abortion and after that, I have become suicidal. I don't know why such a thing happened to me. I have stopped believing in God as I feel I don't deserve to chant the holy name of God, but at the same time I am angry with him for putting me in the worst situation of my life.

Please guide me. I am absolutely broke and I don't know what to do ahead in life as it has become a burden for me.

Dr. Stone's Reply:

Greetings my friend!

Thank you for your question!

There are two ways of thinking in the world and only two. Everyone thinks from their God mind or from what is called the Negative Ego mind, or fear-based mind, or lower-self mind.

Because of lack of proper Spiritual training, which is not your fault, you have let your negative ego mind take over your consciousness. That is why you are experiencing what is called "a dark night of the soul." It is at this time, when you are at rock bottom that you let go of the negative ego and God is allowed through. God has guided you to me for the training you need. God wants me to tell you that He loves you very much. The experiences you went through that were catalysts to make you lose faith and belief in God were Spiritual Tests, which you misinterpreted because you allowed the negative ego mind to misinterpret your lessons. The letting go of God put you under control of the negative ego mind even more and now, finally, you have hit rock bottom. It is not possible to be successful in life without God and without thinking from your God mind. God does not blame you, of course, for He knows you need training. You were not open before, but now He says you are open, and He is very pleased about this. God is going to personally train you how to master your mind and emotions through the study of my books and Website. All the articles on the Website are totally free and will cost you nothing! So you cannot beat that price!

God wishes you to know that you feel you don't deserve because you do not love yourself. I will train you how to do this. You are angry at

God because you are living out of what is called "Victim Consciousness." You are under the faulty belief of the negative ego that God is causing your life, which, in truth, is illusion. You, my friend, are causing your life by how you think! You have let the negative ego mind take over your consciousness and you have allowed yourself to be a victim of your mind and emotions. I will teach you, with God's help, how to master the mind, master your emotions, and get rid of the negative ego so you only think at all times with your Spiritual/Christ/Buddha mind! Then you will see very clearly it is you who, by mistake, misunderstood your Spiritual Tests and lessons by listening to your negative ego mind and not God. Your suffering is a blessing, in truth, for it is the catalyst to push you to write to me—who is a Spiritual Master serving God! All that is needed is a little proper Spiritual training and you will be as good as new! This should be taught in school but is not. So you had to learn the hard way. This is okay, for all is forgiven my friend, and God wishes you to know this. In truth, you are a Son of God and just lost your way a little bit, but like the prodigal Son, He always welcomes his Sons and Daughters back. He is very pleased you are now ready to come back and you have demonstrated this by being willing to put aside the negative ego and write me to receive the Spiritual Training you need! So God wants you to now reclaim you personal power and self-mastery and become a Spiritual Warrior and get up and fight! You will now become a team player and have a co-partnership and get your life back together. Your job is to learn how to think properly, for your emotions are caused by how you think not by anything outside of self. This is a lesson you must learn now! So go to my Website and start studying all the chapters and start doing the free meditations as well. It is all free, so there are no excuses.

Once you start getting back on your feet then I want you to purchase my book *Soul Psychology*, which will greatly help. In that book, you will find affirmations to work with. God wishes you to begin chanting the Holy Names as well. He would be honored if you would do so. He is so pleased you are now coming home and the Angels in Heaven are rejoicing and singing. Look at what has occurred to you as a bad dream, nothing more. You have now reawakened from a bad sleep, and all is well. Forgive self for all mistakes, for everything is just lessons!

Here is the Website address: http://www.drjoshuadavidstone.com Start reading all the articles on the Website of the free chapters of my 31 books. God will read these chapters with you and start turning on all the inner lights in your mind, so to speak. It takes only 21 days to cement a new habit of positive/Spiritual/Christ/Buddha thinking in your mind. You can do it today; however, it will take just 21 days to make positive thinking a habit. So God says go and do your Spiritual Homework as I have suggested which is God speaking to you through the written word. The last thing God wishes to tell you is that you are totally loved and everything is forgiven. Everyone on Earth has lessons to learn and rejoices in the fact that at such a young age you are now learning yours! Everyone learns by the school of hard knocks when they are young! Did not Krishna say to Arjuna in the *Bhagavad-Gita*, "Give up your unmanliness and get up and fight, this self-pity and self-indulgence is unbecoming of the Great Soul that you are"! He is speaking to you, my friend, as he did to Lord Buddha who was Arjuna in a past life! Lord Buddha has become one of our greatest Spiritual Leaders as well, my friend. The thousand-mile journey begins with the first step! Start making it now, says God, and go to Dr. Stone's Website and start studying! God will sit on your shoulder, head, and heart, and study with you! The Light has come! Your karma has now changed! Peace is at hand! The Force is now with you! Praise God, for another one of God's Sons is now returning home!

Warmest Regards,
Dr Joshua David Stone

* *

2

On Impatience, Sadness, Love, and a Sense of Urgency

Dear Dr. Stone,

Well, while appreciating the fact that you are busy for two years, it is disappointing to know that India will have to wait that long for you. Actually, a lot of Spiritualists in India were very excited about your visit and now they are disappointed. Can you not manage to squeeze in one visit to India at least by mid-2002, maybe just to Chennai and not to any other city?

Please try to manifest this, that would probably work just as well as bi-location and tri-location. Maybe you should try multi-location? I am confident that so many souls' requests cannot be ignored by you.

If you don't mind, can I ask a few questions?

After learning a lot, and experiencing a lot of spiritual energy, and doing a lot of healing, what I find in many awakening hearts are feelings that can be best described as:

a) impatience b) sadness c) so much love and compassion that it hurts d)a sense of urgency

Everyone everywhere wants miracle healings for the suffering souls. People expect a magical vanishing of all problems and sufferings and get disturbed seeing what is going on outside in our world. This is itself evidence of the deep compassion and love pulsing in these hearts. But please tell me how can one deal with this, and can one really turn this into a positive healing for Mother Earth and Humanity? Do you also at times feel this overwhelming need to do more, more, and more? Is sadness for others' sufferings justified?

I'm sorry I'm taking up your time. I really need to know when the time will come for everyone to wake up and take responsibility for themselves. Till then I suppose the work has to continue.

Thank you for listening to me and I hope you will give me your answers that will enlighten many souls.

I am still positive that you will come to India next year.

In Spiritual and Unconditional Love and Light

Dr. Stone's Reply

Greetings my Friend!

Thanks for your sweet note! The questions you ask are excellent and I will answer them with the answers your soul seeks!

Impatience and sadness are caused by interpreting life from the negative ego/separative/fear-based mind rather than interpreting our life from the Spiritual/Christ/Buddha/Krishna mind! Many in the world are very attuned Spiritually and very advanced Spiritually but are not as advanced Psychologically! There are three levels to God Realization and this is what a great many Spiritual seekers do not understand. God must be realized Spiritually, Psychologically, and on a Physical/Earthly level. Many try to solve Psychological lessons through Spiritual means and it does not work! All lessons must be mastered at the level of the problem. All feelings and emotions are caused by how a person thinks. I very humbly tell you that is why my work is so important for it teaches not only the highest Spiritual Ascension and Ascended Masters work, but it also teaches the most cutting-edge Psychological work. I also teach physical healing, business, and earthly mastery to people on all levels. Integration is the key! This is why my two books *Soul Psychology* and *How to Release Fear-Based Thinking and Feeling* are so important. For the weak spot in most Spiritual Leaders, Teachers, and Lightworkers is the lack of understanding of the psychological laws of God! By the grace of God, I have a gift for teaching this information in a very easy to understand, practical and cutting-edge style which can be learned as simply as reading my books.

Now in terms of your question about compassion to the point of hurting. This is also a manifestation of the faulty thinking of the negative ego mind. It is why Sai Baba has said, "God equals man minus ego"! To realize God, one must transcend the negative ego mind. In this case, it must be understood that there is a difference between compassion and empathy. Empathy, or being an empath, is a negative ego manifestation where the person takes on the pain of others. God wants people to have compassion but not take on the suffering. This can be related to having a healthy psychological immune system. Just as when one is physically sick—no one would take on the sickness or cold or virus as an act of compassion. Of course a person should stay physically healthy but yet have compassion and try to help those that are not well physically.

The same is true psychologically. When someone has negative feelings and emotions, the ideal is to have a strong psychological immune system and have compassion yes, but not take on the mental or emotional sickness of suffering. Inner peace and happiness is a state of mind; an attitude and perspective on life. That is why the Bible says, "Let this mind be in you that was in Christ Jesus." If you prefer to call this the Buddha mind or Krishna mind, it is the same thing!

Also it must be understood that all suffering comes from attachment, as Buddha said in his Four Noble Truths. You do not want attachment, or non-attachment, or to be to detached. You want "involved detachment." This is the ticket, my friend. Compassion that causes suffering is an attachment. Being too detached is being insensitive and lacking in compassion. "Involved detachment" is the fine balance you seek in this lesson!

Now the sense of urgency can be a good thing or a bad thing. Some times this stems from the Spiritual/Christ/Buddha mind and other times it could be the negative ego mind. So this one needs some Spiritual discernment. People should have a sense of Spiritual urgency to seek God, otherwise they are wasting the incarnation. However, on the other side of the coin, everyone needs to live within the Tao and understand there is a yin and yang to all things. Much like surfing a wave in the ocean. If you go to fast you will get dumped by the wave, if you go too slow you miss the wave. You must remain in the Tao! So both these points must be considered! I feel a need to do more myself and that is why I am so specifically single-pointed in my efforts in having become a Spiritual Master and realized my Ascension and why I am so dedicated in my Service work. What must be understood is that righteousness in the eyes of God is trying! God is not looking for perfection for mistakes are part of life and how we learn. God wishes us to give our best effort, and regardless of the outcome God is pleased!

Now in regard to your question as to whether sadness is ever justified, the answer is "no"! It is never justified! Buddha said all suffering comes from your attachments. All suffering comes from a wrong point of view! Study my books and Website and I will teach you how to think properly which will only create positive Spiritualized feelings and emotions. Sadness does not exist except as a manifestation of faulty thinking within one's own mind. The cause of all problems and suffering is ego or negative ego. This can also be called separation thinking or fear-based thinking!

In terms of the suffering in the world. When one realizes each person is an incarnation of God and God is the only being that exists and that we all share the same identity as the Eternal Self. This does not mean that everyone is at the same level of realization this truth, but in the highest ideal this is the truth. Knowing that you are God and all others are God, then, of course, one wants to be of service. What one gives to another one is literally giving to oneself. One cannot realize God without seeing God in another.

So on the Earthly level of God Realization, everyone has a Spiritual Mission, Spiritual Puzzle Piece, Spiritual Contract, Personal Spiritual Blueprint in the Divine Plan that they are responsible to fulfill! To Realize God on the Physical/Earthly level this must be achieved and fulfilled. As they say in your part of the world, one must fulfill their Dharma! The idea is to not just be God in Heaven, true Ascension is being God in your physical body on Earth. The Spiritual Path is very simple. If you want to be with God in Heaven, then act like God on Earth! Once understanding the importance of manifesting God on Earth and each person's responsibility to try to help relieve the suffering of others and to change our civilization in an Earthly sense into a more Five Dimensional Civilization or Utopian-type of world. The Material world and Earthly Civilization is our responsibility to fix and heal. What else is one to going to do with their time rather than seek Spiritual Growth, help people, and try to make our world a better place! The key, however, is to do this in a way where one is first right with self and right with God within so all the lessons of life do not knock you off center. All these wonderful questions you ask are examples of places where people are not fully right with self and right with God!

This is the polishing of the Diamond that each person must do on themselves to be an effective Spiritual Master and effective servant of the Divine on Earth!

I very humbly and with total humility hope and pray that these humble answers to your questions have been of assitance! This would indeed be a good letter to post for there is much wisdom and insight to be gained through the study of it! I thank you my friend for asking such insightful questions!

Your Eternal Spiritual Brother and Friend!
Dr Joshua David Stone

* *

3

An Invitation to India

Dear Dr. Stone,

Greetings! I am sure that there must be very few great souls like you, who immediately after such a grand Spiritual Event like the Wesak Festival, would find the time or the inclination to reply to each email personally! I can just imagine that the aftermath must be pleasantly exhausting and I cannot thank you enough for replying to me. I am delighted that you are considering visiting India, the birthplace of The Vedas, to share with us your wisdom.

Whenever you find the time in your busy schedule, please do send me your literature about your workshops and seminars. This year, Master Alton will be visiting India to present Level III of The Melchizedek Method, and as an organizer I am committed to this service.

Do you think July or August would be a good time in 2002? I am eager to receive more information from you regarding this.

Thank you, and looking forward to bringing you to this Punya Bhoomi.

In Spiritual and Unconditional Love and Divine Light,

Dr. Stone's Reply:

Greetings my friend!

Thanks for your sweet words. Yes, I take the emailing as a divine service even though it is a lot of work at times. I also enjoy it, for it allows me to connect with very sweet and lovely people like yourself! So I am enriched as well!

As soon as I get the new information packets made I will send one to you. I should have them ready within a month. I want to be sure to give you the new information packet. In the meantime, the Website contains most of the information except for the brand new write-ups that I am working on right now!

I would love to come to India, however, my travel schedule right now is literally booked for the next two years. The success of the books and Wesaks have, by the grace of God and the Masters, given me an overwhelming number of invitations. I am literally booked now for over two years in my travel schedule! Plus, the Masters want me to finish these last nine books to complete my 40 volume Ascension Book Series. If there should be any cancellations or travel changes I will definitely be in touch. I think the only answer is to learn to physically bi-locate or even tri-Locate, which would be even better!

I send you my Warmest Regards and Love,
Dr Joshua David Stone

* *

4

True Happiness will Not come from your Boyfriend

DEAR DR. STONE:

I'M A 23 YEAR-OLD GIRL DEEPLY IN LOVE WITH A CLASS FEL-LOW OF MINE. WE LOVE EACH OTHER, BUT THE CONCERN IS WHETHER WE WILL GET CONSENT FROM HIS PARENTS FOR MARRIAGE. OUT OF AN ATTEMPT OF NOT LOSING HIM, I ENTERED INTO PHYSICAL RELATIONSHIP WITH HIM, WHICH I KNOW WILL NOT BE ACCEPTED WELL BY OUR FAMILIES & SOCIETY. I REMAIN DEPRESSED AT THE THOUGHT OF HIS NOT BEING THERE IN MY LIFE TOMOR-ROW AND, IN FACT, GET THOUGHTS OF COMMITTING SUCIDE. I LOVE HIM ALOT & AM CONFIDENT OF MY ACT BECAUSE IN MY HEART I ACCEPTED HIM AS MY LIFE & TRIED TO GIVE HIM EVERYTHING A WIFE SHOULD DO FOR HER HUSBAND. I JUST DON'T WANT TO LOSE HIM AT ANY COST. I WILL DO ANYTHING TO HAVE HIM AS MY HUSBAND. TELL ME THE WAY BY WHICH I CAN CONVINCE HIM & HIS

PARENTS TO ALLOW US TO TIE THE NUPTIAL KNOT, BECAUSE MY LIFE WITHOUT HIM IS MEANINGLESS & I NEED A REASON TO LIVE A MEANINGFUL & A FULFILLING LIFE AS A DEVOTED WIFE OF HIS.

THANKS.

Dr. Stone's Reply:

Greetings my Friend!

God is guiding you to write to me for he wishes to speak to you through my words, so listen closely.

The fact that you love him is a wonderful thing and God would never want you to lose this. God also wishes you to know how much He loves you! God, however, also wants you to understand that there are two kinds of love. There is a lower self and Higher Self form of love. One is addictive and the other is self-actualized. God, with total love in his heart for you, wishes you to understand that as with most young people your age it is time now to switch from dependent love to independent love in your attitude. You have put all your eggs in one basket (your boyfriend) and not put any eggs, so to speak, in your basket with God or your self. The two most important relationships in your life are not your boyfriend. It is your relationship to self and God!

Lord Buddha has said that all suffering comes from attachment. All suffering comes form wrong points of view. You are too attached to your boyfriend. Everything in life must be a preference, not an attachment. You are so attached you even think thoughts of suicide. This is not a judgment, just a lesson that it is time to self-actualize yourself more. The purpose and goal of life is not to have a boyfriend and get married. The first goal of life should be to realize God or become Self Realized and be of service to the world. Boyfriends and marriage are important, but you have made them too important. Your happiness is in another person rather than in yourself. This is a lesson you need to learn and that is why you are writing me. In truth, that which you attach yourself to in the end you push away. You must go after your preferences in life, however, you must change your attitude to be happy whether you get your preferences or not. This is all controlled by your thinking!

To learn how to reprogram your conscious and subconscious thinking I would recommend reading my book *Soul Psychology*, which you can order on my Website, and you should study my Website with all the free articles. Everyone is searching for happiness and I am going to tell you a great secret here. True happiness is not your boyfriend; it is learning to think with your spiritual mind not your fear-based/lower-self/separative/negative ego mind. This should be taught in school, but unfortunately, it is not. Therefore, God has sent you to me to be trained in how to do this, which I have thus given you. You must divide your love equally between self-love, love for God, and love for your boyfriend, to be balanced. You have given all to your boyfriend and left out self and God! God is now gently and lovingly reminding you of this, not in a critical way, but in the sweet voice of Love!

Follow my guidance and it will save you much suffering in life and is the key also to more likely getting what you want! Also, do not forget to pray. Time to bring God into your life. Things are not working for you have left God out of the equation. Study my book and Website! (http://www.drjoshuadavidstone.com)

Warmest Regards,
Dr Joshua David Stone

* *

5

On Destiny

Hello Dr. Stone,

I am very much intrigued by the phenomenon called "Destiny." It is said that God knows everything of the past, present and even the FUTURE!!! of every living entity. From that, my small intellect concludes that the future is already set and is unchangeable. So, when people say that we can shape our own destiny, it seems to be wrong. What is your answer to this query Dr. Stone?

Dr. Stone's Reply:

Greetings my friend!

Thank you for your most important question. This is an issue that is confusing to a great many people on the Earth, so it is very good that you have asked this. It is actually one of the most important questions anyone can ask!

Spirit and the inner plane Ascended Masters would answer your question in this manner. It must be understood that all you have stated in your question is true about God having all knowledge of past, present and future; however, there is just one piece of the puzzle you are missing in your understanding that will bring the proper integration you seek. It is also true that we each cause our own reality by how we think! Our thoughts cause our feelings, emotions, energy, behavior, and what we attract and magnetize into our life!

So it must be understood that God has given each of us, as Sons and Daughters of God, free choice! Life is not just God doing everything for us; it is also a co-creation. So to understand the future it can be seen as kind of like the grid of a checkerboard. The future grid is set as you have so insightfully stated. However, the other key insight that must be understood is that even though the grid is set, the checkerboard squares are not. Those are filled in by each person's free choice! So it would not be true to say that everything is set. In truth, except for this basic grid, we do create our own destiny. It was insightful of you to tune into the this grid, however, to find the proper integration and balance, it is important for every person on Earth to fully own their personal power, free choice, and to take total control of their life. In the West there is a saying, "God helps those who help themselves." So the way to live properly is to see life as a co-creation. Pray to God and the inner plane Masters of the East and West for help, and then own your personal power and positive thinking and do everything in your power to create your preferences in life. Notice I used the word "preferences" rather than "attachments"! Did not Buddha say in his Four Noble Truths that all suffering comes from attachments? A preference is an attitude that allows you to go after what you want with all your heart and soul and mind and might, however, if you don't get it, you are still happy! This, my dear insightful friend, is the integration and balance you seek!

Warmest Regards
Dr Joshua David Stone

* *

6

It's Good to Learn from GOD in All Forms

Dear Dr. Stone:

I am really delighted to read your achievements of the spiritual world. I am also a serious student of this ultimate world though I have not yet written my experiences in any book but I wish to do so soon. I am interested to read about your work as I feel that the more you share your experiences, the more one moves ahead in enlightenment as one gets to know more of spiritualism, abode of GOD, where everyone is free from death and birth. I hope you understand what I mean because you must be aware that such experiences are difficult to put in words.

With regards,

Dr. Stone's Reply:

Greetings my friend!

Thank you for your comments and very kind words. They are most appreciated!

Everyone in life has a Spiritual mission, dharma, puzzle piece and/or personal blueprint and Spiritual Contract in the Divine Plan of God and the Masters! What is most important in life is to fulfill this Spiritual puzzle piece to the best of your ability. As you have stated, one of my humble gifts is the ability to put into clear easy to understand words, that which a great many Spiritual seekers are experiencing on the Path. Keep studying these teachings for they will take you to the Promised Land you seek, both in consciousness and in a literal sense. Take advantage of the gifts of your brothers and sisters, just as you share your gifts with others! For each person on Earth is, in truth, an incarnation of God! It is good to learn from God in all forms. You have clearly stated your openness and willingness to do this both in a giving and receiving sense, which is good my friend! Spirit and the Masters are pleased!

Warmest Regards,
Dr Joshua David Stone

* *

7

"I Cannot Concentrate— Please Help!"

Dear Dr. Stone:

I am a mentally distressed 16 -year-old girl. I hope you will listen to a disappointed girl and bring her out of her distress. PLEASE SIR, HELP ME. I feel nervous during exams and cannot really concentrate. I keep on getting negative thoughts. The basic problem is that I cannot concentrate. Please bestow me with some tips on how to concentrate. I have a lot of queries, but I am afraid that you may not hear me, a humble girl of 16 years.

Please help me. I need your help or I may have a nervous breakdown.

Dr. Stone's Reply:

Greetings, my Sweet friend!

God listens to the heartfelt prayers of all, especially those with a humble heart! Spirit and the Masters wish to help you through me. Listen closely to my guidance and you will quickly and easily heal!

Your mental distress, nervousness, negative thoughts, inability to concentrate and fear about a nervous breakdown are caused by one thing and one thing alone. They are caused by the fact that no one has trained you how to master and control your own mind and feelings and emotions! This should be taught in school and is not. So do not feel bad about this for it is not your fault! However, it is your responsibility to master this lesson. I shall quickly and easily teach you how! Please listen closely!

First you must understand that your thoughts create your reality. These exams are not causing you any problems; it is your negative thinking that is. There are only two ways to think in the world and only two. You either think with your Spiritual/Krishna/Christ/Buddha/Positive/Love mind, or your Fear-based/separative/lower-self/negative ego/selfish/maya mind! This is why Sai Baba has stated the definition of God is, "God equals man minus ego"! Ego here being the negative thinking of this false mind!

Secondly you must understand your feelings do not come from people or anything outside of self. They come from how you think! Did not Lord Buddha say in his Four Noble Truths, "All suffering comes from wrong points of view"? There is absolutely nothing wrong with you, my sweet friend, just a little faulty thinking which is creating negative feelings within you. This is easily cured by gaining more mastery of your mind.

What I want you to do is every time a negative thought comes into your mind push it out of your mind and replace it with a positive thought or image! I want you to constantly tell yourself from now on you are the Master of all your thoughts, feelings, emotions, energy, and physical body!

A famous Spiritual Teacher in the West by the name of Edgar Cayce said, "Why worry when you can pray"! I also want you to pray to God (Brahma) and your favorite Spiritual Masters. Krishna, Rama, Vishnu, Shiva, Buddha, Jesus, the Divine Mother, Quan Yin, Mother Mary, or whoever else you want, and ask them all for help. Pray constantly. Ask them also to remove all negative thoughts and feelings from your consciousness! God, the Masters and your own Personal Power and willpower, pushing the negative thoughts out of your mind and replacing them with positive thoughts, will instantly make you feel better! You also must never have attachments, only preferences. Your disappoint comes from attachments, which is the cause of all suffering. Have very strong preferences, which is an attitude that allows you to be happy whether you get your preferences or not! Your lack of concentration is because you are not owning your personal power and will power, and taking control of your mind and emotions. You are letting the subconscious mind run you instead of your being 100% in control of your subconscious mind! You are the computer programmer, however, you are letting the computer run the programmer instead of being the programmer of your computer. It only takes 21 days to cement a new habit into your subconscious mind. If you practice what I say for 21 days, you will have a habit of being happy and peaceful instead of feeling bad as you have described!

It has been my great honor, my sweet friend, to serve as an instrument of God and your Angels to teach you this lesson. Just as you have lessons in school, God has certain lessons he would like you to learn as well! This is one of them! One last technique I shall give you is to chant the name of God and your favorite Spiritual Masters when negative thoughts try to get in, or any time you like! There is a saying in the West, "An idle mind is the devil's workshop"! If you fill your mind with God thoughts, images, feelings, actions and behaviors, there will be no room for the negative mind to get in and after 21 days you will have a habit of being able to concentrate and be happy! Ask your parents to buy you my book *Soul Psychology*, for this book will give you much explanation and provide even more easy to understand techniques. Also, read all the free articles on my Website if you have access to a computer and the Internet. If not, have your parents just buy the book for you! This is a great blessing that you are going to learn these lessons at such an early age! God and the Masters bless you and want you to know they greatly love you!

Your humble Spiritual Servant and Friend!
Dr Joshua David Stone

* *

8

On a Marriage Proposal

Dear Dr. Stone:

I have a friend, who about a month back proposed for marriage and we decided to work toward a better future and see if the things can work out between us. Suddenly she has stopped communicating and has not given any reason for such behavior. I am feeling uncomfortable about the whole thing. How should I take it?

Dr. Stone's Reply:

Greetings my friend!

Thanks for your question. There is a famous saying in the West that "Communication is to a relationship what breathing is to living"! What needs to be done is you need to ask her why she has stopped communicating and ask if there is anything bothering her. Relationships are like a beautiful garden. Weeds often grow and it is essential to pull out these weeds which occur in every relationship; before they overgrow the beautiful flowers that represent your love.

There may be nothing wrong, but it is always good to check. The lesson is to ask her directly! It may be an internal lesson having nothing to do with you or it may be some anger, judgment, or something bothering her. Asking her to share without any defensiveness on your part and letting her get out her thoughts and feelings whatever the cause, will promote healing! This is the guidance you seek, my friend!

Warmest Regards,
Dr Joshua David Stone

* *

9

What to do when in a Dilemma

Dear Dr. Stone:

What to do when you are in a dilemma?

Dr. Stone's Reply:

Greetings my friend!

This is a good question. When you are in a dilemma there are a number of things you need to do! The first is to fully claim your personal power, inner strength, and Spiritual Warrior attitude!

Secondly, remember that all dilemmas are Spiritual Tests, and that God is testing you and you should develop a great Spiritual desire to pass this Spiritual test!

Next, pray to God, the inner plane Ascended Masters for help in resolving this dilemma!

Lastly, make a Spiritual Battleplan of everything you can do using your own personal power, actions and abilities to resolve this situation! By doing this, your own God-given creative mind and God's mind will help you to resolve this situation! This, my friend, is the Secret of the Ages to resolving all dilemmas!

Read the free articles on my Website (http://www.drjoshuadavid-stone.com) for more in-depth help in such matters!

Warmest regards and love,
Dr Joshua David Stone

* *

10

"What Obstructs One's Path to Self-Realization?"

Dear Dr. Stone:

How to check obstruction in the goal of Self-Realization?

Dr. Stone's Reply:

Greetings my friend!

Thanks for your most wonderful question! There is only one obstruction on the path to Self-Realization and that is what is called "ego" or "negative ego," and "imbalance"! All problems and/or lessons in life stem from this and only this! Ego or negative ego could also be termed the fear-based mind, selfishness, illusion, maya, glamour, misperception and/or misthinking and feeling! Everyone on earth thinks from their God mind or the small, self-centered ego mind! Ego could also be most clearly called the separative mind. In truth, it does not really even exist. It is a fabrication of the misuse of free choice that God has given us! In the West, it is called the eating of the fruit of the "Tree of Good and Evil"!

So my good friend, to check obstruction to the goal of Self-Realization be Spiritually vigilant over controlling your negative ego mind and emotions! To learn how to do this read my books *Soul Psychology*, *How to Release Fear-Based Thinking and Feeling*, and study the free articles on my Website! This is the answer you seek, my friend!

Warmest regards and Love on your Spiritual Journey!
Dr Joshua David Stone

* *

11

On the Conflict between Marriage and Career

Dear Dr. Stone:

What should a person do when there arises a conflict in his mind, especially between marriage and career?

Dr. Stone's Reply:

Greetings my friend!

This is a very good question and a very tough question! You are asking a question here that is really going to have to put your friend Dr Joshua to work here. For there is no pat answer to this question for each situation in life is unique and different depending on personal circumstance.

This being said I would answer your question this way, my thoughtful friend. One's first obligation in life is to be right with self and right with God! Said another way, one's first responsibility is to God and one's Spiritual path. This is why you have incarnated into this physical body and into this world, which is to achieve Self-Realization. Part of one's Spiritual Path is to be of Service to your Brothers and Sisters. So part of the answer to this question depends on how important this job is to you and how much it is a part of your Spiritual path. If it is just a job to make money then maybe more flexibility is appropriate. The sacred vows of marriage are also very important. This is a bond that one hopefully makes for one's entire life. This is nothing to be taken lightly. So the answer I would give is in every situation of life one must keep the proper "Selfish and Selfless balance"! There is a time in life to be selfish and a time to be more selfless! Do not be selfish when the lesson is to be selfless and do not be selfless when it is time to be more Spiritually selfish!

Another key to making the right decision is to weigh the intensity of the feelings you have and your spouse has. If one is much stronger then the other in intensity this may be an answer as well.

Thirdly, pray to God and ask for guidance!

Fourthly make a list of the pros and cons on a piece of paper for the act of writing it on paper will help to clarify this decision in your mind.

Last, be open to balance and compromise if need be. However, above all else, to thine own Self be True! If conflict still remains, just pray to God and ask for God to make the correct decision for you!

This is the answer you seek, my friend! You might enjoy my books *Ascension and Romantic Relationships* and *Your Ascension Mission: Embracing your Puzzle Piece* for further clarification!

Warmest Regards and Love,
Dr Joshua David Stone

* *

12

On the Planetary Ascension Movement and Ascended Master Teachings

Dear Dr. Stone:

Can you please give some more information on the Planetary Ascension Movement and Ascended Master Teachings? I shall be greatly appreciative.

Thanks,

Dr. Stone's Reply:

Greetings my friend!

You ask a big question, my friend! I have written 31 books on this question. To answer this question in a nutshell is no easy task! I shall do my best!

The best answer is can give you is this. The Ascended Masters are those Spiritual beings who live in the Spiritual world from all religions who have achieved liberation from the wheel of rebirth however continue to serve to help their brothers and sisters on Earth! They also make up the true Spiritual Government of this planet!

Ascension is the process whereby each person merges and integrates on earth with their Mighty I Am Presence (Monad) and Higher Self! This can also be called achieving and passing their seven levels of Initiation which all souls must pass to achieve liberation from the wheel of rebirth!

The first dispensation of Ascended Master Teachings were those of Madam Blavatsky and the Theosophical Movement. The Second Dispensation was that of the Alice Bailey Teachings and the Channelings of the Ascended Master Djwhal Khul. Thirdly was the I AM Teachings of Saint Germain through Godfre Ray King. The Fourth Dispensation of Ascended Master Teachings brought forth to this planet is the 40 volume Ascension Book Series I have humbly brought forth to the planet which is a synthesis of the best of the past and brings forth brand new cutting-edge Ascended Master teachings. What is also unique about this work is its emphasis on synthesis and integration and the importance of learning to achieve God Realization on a Spiritual, Psychological and Physical/Earthly level. God must be realized Spiritually, mentally, emotionally, energetically, and physically, in an Earthly sense. I very humbly say my work is unique in that I teach how to do this on all levels, not just in one, in an integrated and balanced manner.

The Planetary Ascension Movement is the fastest growing Spiritual Movement in the entire world and I like to call it "The Rocketship to God," for this is truly what it is. In my very humble opinion all paths to God are beautiful, however, there is no faster path and method to God realization then the Teachings of the Ascended Masters of all religions! Especially read my books *The Complete Ascension Manual* and *Soul Psychology* for the best initial overview of this work!

Warmest Regards and Love,
Dr Joshua David Stone

* *

13

Letter to GOD and the Masters

from Joshua

I JOSHUA AND WE NOW OFFICIALLY CALL FORTH AN OFFI-
CIAL COUNCIL MEETING WITH THE! BELOVED PRESENCE
OF GOD, CHRIST, HOLY SPIRIT, MELCHIZEDEK, MAHATMA,
METATRON, ARCHANGEL MICHAEL, ARCHANGEL GABRIEL,
DIVINE MOTHER, SAI BABA, LORD OF ARCTURUS, HELIOS
AND VESTA, COMMANDER ASHTAR, MOTHER MARY, QUAN
YIN, LORD BUDDHA, LORD MAITREYA, SAINT GERMAIN,
ALLAH GOBI, MASTER KUTHUMI, EL MORYA, MASTER SER-
APIS BEY, PAUL THE VENETIAN, MASTER HILARION, LADY
PORTIA, DJWAHL KHUL AND SANANDA,

MY BELOVED FRIENDS!

THE NIGHT BEFORE LAST I GOT SOME EXTREMELY
STRONG DREAM GUIDANCE FROM YOU CONCERNING
WHAT YOU TOLD ME IN A VERY CLEAR AND DECISIVE
MANNER OF MY RESPONSIBILITY TO A CERTAIN EXTENT
AND DEGREE FOR THE POTENTIAL OUTCOME OF WORLD

EVENTS ON THIS PLANET. THESE WERE NOT THE EXACT
WORDS YOU USED FOR I CANNOT REMEMBER THEM
EXACTLY BUT THIS WAS THE BASIC VERY CLEAR GUID-
ANCE AND DIRECTION I WAS GIVEN!

I HAVE CALLED FORTH THIS COUNCIL MEETING TO VERY
CLEARLY TELL YOU THAT I HAVE RECEIVED THIS GUIDANCE
QUITE CLEARLY AND I VERY HUMBLY AND JOYFULLY TAKE
ON THIS "MANTLE OF RESPONSIBILITY" IN THIS REGARD!
THERE ARE MANY WAYS I HAVE ALREADY PUT THIS INTO
MOTION AND AFTER THIS VERY CLEAR DREAM GUIDANCE, I
HAVE INSTITUTED SOME OTHERS AS WELL!

AT PLATINUM WESAK AS YOU KNOW I AM GOING TO BE
DOING FOR THE FIRST TIME MY INTENSIVE WORLD SER-
VICE WORK IN MY ACTUAL MEDITATIONS AT THE END
AND FOR THE FIRST TIME I WILL BE INTRODUCING THE
GLOBAL WORLD SERVICE HUNA PRAYERS TO THE GROUP
WHICH SHOULD BE QUITE POWERFUL AND EFFECTIVE
WITH YOUR HELP!

I HAVE ALSO CREATED A NEW SECTION ON THE ACADEMY
WEBSITE CALLED "GLOBAL WORLD SERVICE PRAYERS TO
TURN THE TIDE OF WORLD EVENTS!" I PUT THE ECONOMY
HUNA PRAYER UP THERE LAST WEEK! I WILL BE ADDING
MORE NEW ONES EACH TIME I WRITE THEM. I ALSO HAVE
ONE OF THE HUNA PRAYERS FOR PEACE FOR THE MIDDLE
EAST ON THE WEBSITE AS WELL!

I HAVE ALSO PUT ALMOST MY ENTIRE BOOK MANUAL FOR
SPIRITUAL LEADERSHIP ON THE WEBSITE WHICH DEALS WITH
THE ASCENDED MASTERS' VIEW ON ALL THE DIFFERENT

POLITICAL, SOCIAL, AND PHILOSOPHICAL ISSUES OF THE EARTH, WHICH I THINK IS QUITE IMPACTFUL!

I WILL ALSO BE MUCH MORE SPIRITUALLY VIGILANT IN A GLOBAL SENSE AS I AM PERSONALLY TO MAKE SURE ANY EARTHLY AREA THAT NEEDS HELP WILL GET IT THROUGH THESE COLLECTIVE MEANS!

I AM ALSO GOING TO SOON WRITE THE BOOK *THE DIVINE PLAN AND BLUEPRINT FOR THE SEVENTH AGE* TO ADD TO THIS PROCESS! I HAVE ALREADY COMPLETED ONE OF THE CHAPTERS OF THE SEVEN RAY PLAN!

I ALSO OFFER MYSELF IN SERVICE IN REGARD TO THE EXTRATERRESTRIAL, POSSIBLE ARCHANGELIC AND EVEN ASCENDED MASTER POSSIBLE VISITATION AT A FUTURE WESAK. I FULLY REALIZE THAT THIS IS NOT IN THE CARDS OR IS EXTREMELY UNLIKELY AT THIS PLATINUM WESAK, HOWEVER, I DO SENSE IT IS A POSSIBILITY AT A FUTURE WESAK AND I OFFER MYSELF AND THE WESAK CELEBRATION TO YOU IN THIS REGARD.

THEN OF COURSE THE SPIRITUAL LEADERSHIP CONFERENCE EACH YEAR AT WESAK IS A VERY IMPORTANT PART OF THIS SERVICE!

I HAVE ALSO ADDED TO THE WEBSITE A SECTION CALLED "THE SPIRITUAL POLITICAL SERVICE" SECTION. WHENEVER I SEE IMPORTANT ISSUES OVER THE INTERNET THAT COME TO ME, I HAVE KAREN PUT THEM IN THIS SECTION TO HELP

RAISE CONSCIOUSNESS—LIKE THE RAINFORESTS, ABUSE OF WOMEN IN AFGHANISTAN, AND SO ON!

I ALSO TRY TO WATCH A LOT OF NEWS AND I WILL DO SO EVEN MORE CLOSELY IN THE FUTURE NOW AFTER RECEIVING THIS GUIDANCE TO MAKE SURE I AM ON TOP OF EVERYTHING THAT IS GOING ON!

THE 40 VOLUME ASCENSION BOOK SERIES WHICH I AM GOING TO TRY AND COME CLOSE TO COMPLETING NEXT YEAR IS ALSO A BIG PART OF THIS AS WELL, FOR THE OVERALL SPIRITUAL EDUCATION CANNOT BE SEPARATED FROM THIS PROCESS AS WELL. I HAVE COMPLETED 31 VOLUMES IN MY ASCENSION BOOK SERIES NOW!

AFTER PLATINUM WESAK AND ONCE I GOT THE NEW WESAK REORGANIZED, I AM PLANNING ON WRITING FIVE NEW BOOKS. THESE ARE REVELATIONS OF GOD AND THE MASTERS VOLUME ONE AND TWO, ASCENSION PSYCHOLOGY VOLUME ONE AND TWO, AND QUESTIONS AND ANSWERS ON THE PATH OF ASCENSION.

THE FIRST FOUR I MENTIONED ARE GOING TO BE INCREDIBLE AND I VERY HUMBLY SAY MAY BE MY BEST BOOKS EVER. I HAVE BEEN WRITING DOWN ALL MY IDEAS FOR AN ENTIRE YEAR EVERY DAY FOR THE FINAL NINE VOLUMES. AND THE BEST IDEAS FOR THE CHAPTERS, OF THE ABOUT 1000 THAT I CAME UP WITH WHICH ARE ALL REALLY GREAT, WILL MAKE UP THESE FIRST FOUR BOOKS. THESE WILL BE THE CREAM OF THE CROP CHAPTERS, ABOUT 200 OF WHICH CAN'T MISS, AND MY VERY BEST CHANNELINGS AND WRITINGS! I AM REALLY INCREDIBLY EXCITED ABOUT THIS. I HAVE

NEVER SPENT AN ENTIRE YEAR BRAINSTORMING IDEAS FOR A SERIES OF BOOKS LIKE THIS. THE BEST OF THESE CHAPTERS WILL ALL GO ON THE WEBSITE AS WELL!

AS YOU HAVE NOTICED AS WELL THIS YEAR, I HAVE ADDED AN INCREDIBLE AMOUNT OF NEW STUFF TO THE WEBSITE! I REALLY FEEL QUITE HUMBLY THAT THE WEBSITE NOW IS REALLY QUITE EXTRAORDINARY.

SO I SHARE THIS ALL WITH YOU TODAY MY FRIENDS, AND FILE THIS REPORT TO JUST EMPHASIZE AGAIN THAT I VERY CLEARLY GOT THE DREAM GUIDANCE THE NIGHT BEFORE LAST AND AGAIN I SAY, I FULLY JOYFULLY ACCEPT THIS MANTLE OF MY RESPONSIBILITY TO A CERTAIN EXTENT AND DEGREE FOR THE POTENTIAL OUTCOME OF WORLD EVENTS ON THIS PLANET THAT YOU HAVE CLEARLY ASKED ME AND GUIDED ME TO TAKE ON AND I FULLY JOYFULLY ACCEPT AND I JUST WANT YOU TO KNOW THAT I HAVE HEARD YOUR GUIDANCE LOUD AND CLEAR AND "I AM ON THE JOB!"

IF THERE ARE ANY OTHER WAYS THAT YOU WOULD LIKE ME TO BE OF SERVICE IN THIS REGARD I JUST WANT YOU TO KNOW THAT I AM AT ALL OF YOUR SERVICE! JUST LET ME KNOW WHATEVER YOU WANT ME TO DO AND I WILL DO WHAT I CAN TO THE BEST OF MY ABILITIES.

THERE IS A LOT MORE I WISH TO TALK TO YOU ABOUT AFTER PLATINUM WESAK ON A LOT OF DIFFERENT FRONTS. HOWEVER, FOR TODAY, I THINK THIS COMPLETES ALL THAT I NEED TO CONSCIOUSLY SAY AND REPORT!

I THANK YOU FOR YOUR DREAM GUIDANCE THE NIGHT BEFORE LAST AND I, OF COURSE, ALWAYS WELCOME IT IN ALL WAYS AND ALL THINGS! I AM ETERNALLY IN YOUR SERVICE!

MUCH, MUCH LOVE,
JOSHUA

* *

14

"I Have Weird Feelings and Intuitions about this Person"

Dear Dr. Stone:

I have these weird feelings/intuitions about someone, which comes out to be true. I think it's my inner voice that compels me to do things/take actions. It is very strong. I feel so scared sometimes. What do I do? Recently I have stopped talking to that person and the feelings have subsided. Still, when I think about him it keeps coming back. What is it? Please help.

Dr. Stone's Reply:

Greetings my friend!

Thank you for your question.

These intuitions and feelings you are getting is the "Still, Small Voice Within" and your Spiritual and psychic senses giving you information.

It is important to learn to trust this information. This person would seem to have some negative ego programming they have not worked out and Spirit is guiding you to stay away from them. By stay away I mean to not contact them physically or even think about them. It is important in life to have boundaries at times with certain people both physically and psychologically. This does not mean you are not unconditionally loving, it is just the proper balance of the Three-Fold Flame of Love, Wisdom and Power! To be able to trust your Spiritual guidance it is important to learn to control your own negative ego/fear-based mind. I am not saying you didn't in this situation, I am just saying this is an important lesson in general. To learn how to do this, study my books *Soul Psychology*, *How to Release Fear-Based Thinking and Feeling*, and *How to Clear the Negative Ego*! Also check the free articles on the Website to get trained more deeply in this work of how to do this!

Keep up the good work!

Warmest Regards and Love,
Dr Joshua David Stone

* *

15

On the Difference between Religion and Spirituality

Dear Dr. Stone:

What's the difference between religion and spirituality? Kindly elaborate.

Regards,

Dr. Stone's Reply:

Greetings my friend!

Thanks for your most interesting question. Religion is a beautiful and most important aspect of Earth life. In God's eyes there will always be a need for the many different religions and God sees them as all leading to the same place. They bring the teachings of God to a great many people. Unfortunately however, many of the traditional religions have been contaminated by misinterpretations of the negative ego or separative mind, which have brought forth a type of false doctrine. A type of God made in man's image, instead of man made in God's image. This has caused a great many people to leave traditional religion and seek Spirituality, which is more one's "inner direct experience" of God and the Masters and not needing an externalized priest or minister to interpret God or sacred scripture for them. In the Seventh Golden Age in the future, religions will be cleansed and healed of this negative ego contamination and more of their true glory will be brought back. Spirituality recognizes that the true church of God lives within your own heart!

I hope this helps, my friend!

Warmest Regards and Love,
Dr Joshua David Stone

* *

16

On A Course in Miracles

Greetings my friend!

Thanks for your email!

With no judgment intended, you have some faulty thinking going on. What *A Course in Miracles* says about attack defense is totally true, but having protection up is not defensive, it is protection. They are two different concepts. When someone attacks you, you must not let it immediately lodge in your subconscious or you will react. You must let it slide off your bubble like water off a duck's back. This is what allows you to respond instead of react. If you react you are in your negative ego. Protection is connected with appropriate detachment and Spiritual discernment. You are confusing words and concepts.

Secondly, we are perfect, as *A Course in Miracles* says, however, we are not perfect in realization of Truth. That is why everyone must go through the process of realizing their 352 levels of initiation. Do not fall into the trap of believing that just because you are the Christ that there is nothing for you to realize. The Heavenly Ideal which is what

A Course in Miracles is teaching, is totally different from the process of Realizing that ideal which *A Course in Miracles* does not talk about. I wrote a book on the proper way to interpret *A Course in Miracles*. Ninety-nine percent of all lightworkers get totally confused by this book, as I did at first. It is one of the best books ever written, but most confusing as well. Read my book, which explains the proper way to interpret it. Spirit and Masters have guided you to write me because the negative ego is misinterpreting *A Course in Miracles* in your mind and this is creating conflict. Trust in what I am saying, for it comes from Sananda himself! I mean that literally! For I have discussed this with him extensively.

Warmest Regards,
Dr Joshua David Stone

* *

The next long awaited "2002 IRIDESCENT DIAMOND HEART WESAK"—CONTACTING AND PROTOTYPING A GALACTIC REALITY—TAKING YOUR SEAT AT THE HIGH COUNCIL will be April 26th through April 28th, 2002! We are now taking registrations! The cost is only $250 if you register in advance, and will be $300 shortly! We just returned from Platinum Wesak, which turned out to be the best Wesak ever! This is guaranteed to be the Spiritual experience of a lifetime!

Of all the books I have written in my Ascension Book Series, I humbly submit the following two books, are the best books I have ever written. They are my Spiritual Masterpieces of all my books, and if you will, my personal Sistine Chapels, if you know what I mean. If you read these books, I personally guarantee you that you will never be the same. They are my life's works I feel! I never enjoyed channeling and writing any two books more than I did these two books. The first one is called *The Golden Book of Melchizedek: How to be an Integrated Christ/Buddha in this Lifetime*! The second book is called *How to Release Fear-Based Thinking and Feeling: An In-depth Study of Spiritual Psychology*! Both of these books are around 700 pages. *The Golden Book of Melchizedek* is my Masterpiece "Integrated book" on the Spiritual path! It is 80 Chapters. *The How to Release Fear-Based Thinking: An In-depth Study of Spiritual Psychology* is 105 Chapters. I humbly say to you, it is one of the most profound books ever written on the subject of Spiritual Psychology, how to release the negative ego, releasing negative feelings and emotions, in an easy to understand and practical manner. Both of these books are electrifying reading! I literally put my heart and soul into both of them, for I wanted them to be my definitive works! They are also two or three years in the making! Anyone reading these books will go through a Spiritual transformation "that truly passeth understanding"!

Also available is another book I just completed called *The Ascended Masters' Perspective on the Basic Lessons of A Course in Miracles*! This is a small book which I let one of my assistants read when I finished it, and she told me it was the most profound book she has ever read! I will let that speak for itself. This book is $20 and $5 for shipping in the United States, Canada $7, $10 in Europe and $20 in Australia!

The next book which is now available is called *The Soul's Perspective on How to Achieve Perfect Radiant Health: A Compilation*! This book is a compilation of all my best chapters from all my 27 volumes on how to achieve perfect radiant health. Most books written on health just deal with it from the physical perspective. This book deals with how to achieve perfect radiant health in the physical body, from a Spiritual, mental, emotional, etheric and physical perspective. I have so many students and friends dealing with physical health lessons that I was guided to write this book and compile this book for people who want to refine and increase their physical health, and who are having health lessons. It is guaranteed to have an enormous effect! I want to emphasize that all four of these books are only available from the Academy and they are not available from any bookstore on this planet. They can be ordered through my secured server service on my Website, or by phone 818 706 8458, by fax 818 706 8540, or by personal check in the United States, or by a Cashiers Check or Postal Money Order in United States dollars if ordering from anywhere outside the United States. I humbly submit that I believe you can intuitively and energetically sense the profundity and enormous value of these newest channeled books brought forth by Spirit, the Masters and myself! Please tell all your friends about them! This is their official unveiling to the public at large!

The fifth book, which is now available, is a book that Wistancia and I have co-authored called *Empowerment and Integration Through The Goddess*! It is another Channeled Master Thesis on the incredible importance of how both women and men can integrate the "Divine Mother and Goddess energies into their lives." This may be the most comprehensive in-depth study of this subject ever put together in written form from the perspective of the Divine Mother, Lady Masters and Ascended Masters themselves! This book is over 600 pages! Guaranteed to totally transform your consciousness as only the Divine Mother and Goddess energies can. Absolutely exhilarating reading! It shares how to become empowered and how to integrate the Divine Mother and the Goddess energies in a very easy to understand and practical manner! This book is absolutely must reading for all who Love the Divine Mother and want to fully integrate the Goddess energies into themselves, in a totally empowered, balanced and unconditionally loving manner!

The next newest book is my first full color illustrated children's book called *The Little Flame and Big Flame*! It is a most wonderful children's book that is really for adults as well, which teaches children of all ages how to let go of the fear-based/selfish/separative/lower-self and how to breath in the Love-based/Spiritual/Higher Self attitude and emotional system in a way and manner both children and adults can understand! Each page is filled with the most glorious colored illustrations, which children will want to read and look through again and again! This book is also a most wonderful Spiritual and Psychological educational tool to train children how to think and feel with the Spiritual/Christ/Buddha mind and not their negative ego/fear-based/separative mind! Also serves as a wonderful gift to children and to parents and people who have care of children! This book was specifically written to help parents and adult caretakers to help train children in this most important area of psychospiritual development, in a way that will be most enjoyable and fun to children and adults alike! The cost of this book is $25, plus $5 for shipping and handling in the United States. Shipping and handling for these books in Canada is $7, Europe is $10. Shipping and Handling for these books to Australia/New Zealand is $20

My seventh book that is now available is called *Ascension Activation Meditations of the Spiritual Hierarchy—A Compilation*! This is a most wonderful book that is a compilation of all my best Ascension Activations in my Ascension Book Series and contains 13 new Ascension Activation Meditations that have not been seen before! Truly a prized possession to have all my best meditations in one sacred volume! This book is guaranteed to accelerate your Ascension process a thousandfold!

My eighth new book, I very humbly state, is one of the most profound books I have ever written! It is called *The Full Spectrum Prism*

Synthesis Bible: Wisdom Quotes of the Masters of all Religions and all Spiritual Paths! This book contains exactly what the title states. The best "Wisdom Quotes" this world has ever known of all religions and all Spiritual paths. All Bibles of all religions are wonderful. This most unique book is literally a "Synthesis Bible" of the best wisdom quotes in my Ascension Book Series and of all religions and all paths back to God! It has been my greatest joy to write this book and one that has taken an enormous amount of work to put together. It is guaranteed to transform your consciousness. The wisdom quotes contained within will come back to you like mantras in times of need to keep you centered, clear and totally within an efficient perception of reality, as God would have it be! Totally electrifying Spiritual reading! I very humbly say I am very proud of this book. I do not believe a "Synthesis Bible" has ever been written on this planet before! Must reading for all lightworkers! You will enjoy it immensely! This book is guaranteed to accelerate your Ascension process a thousandfold!

I had a dream recently after writing these new series of books and getting them prepared to be made available to the public. In the dream I saw all of these new books waiting to be sent out to people who ordered them. In the dream each book being sent out was in a very sacred box, and covered in a beautiful blue velvet cloth that looked just like the "Torah" or the sacred writings in Jewish temple! In the dream, every person receiving these books was receiving them encased in this etheric energy design! After the dream I knew that this was exactly how I inwardly felt about these books. People will not be receiving them physically in a sacred box with velvet cloth surrounding them like the sacred writing of the "Torah" or "Kabballah," however, energetically and etherically this is exactly what you will be receiving. I put my heart and soul into these books and this is the symbol I received from Spirit as to the sacredness of that which all who read these books will be receiving!

All of the books mentioned in this letter are available from the Academy by email, phone, fax, and can be paid for by credit card, personal check in the United States, and Cashiers Check or Postal Money order in United States Dollars outside of the United States!

For information on all my books, visit the Academy Website: http://www.drjoshuadavidstone.com

All books are sent out the day we receive the order. Payment can be made by credit card or check. Orders in United States should receive books literally within two or three days.

I would also recommend obtaining my audio Ascension Activation Meditation Tapes. Most of these tapes were done live at the Wesak Celebrations in Mt. Shasta with over 1500 to 2000 people in attendance. The activations on these tapes are so powerful and profound that I humbly suggest you will find nothing like them. All of these tapes will blow your mind! They are designed to work perfectly in an experiential manner with the books and Wesak to give you one of the most profound training courses in Spiritual Psychology and Ascension Training ever given forth to this planet! I recommend working with one tape a day and then on the seventh day resting! The combination of the books with the experiential aspect of the tapes and then Wesak I like to call the "Rocketship to God!"

Please also consider getting some channeled sessions with the Ascended Masters from my wife Wistancia. I would highly recommend getting 1. Implant and Negative Elemental Session. 2. Initiation, Light Quotient and Ray Reading, and 3. Ascension Clearing Session. Sessions are $100 per session and can be done by audio cassette tape or over the phone. To receive a session email Wistancia at wistancia@charter.net or call her at 818 706 8533.

You can order or register by credit card or personal check. If by credit card you can do it over my secured server service on my Website, or over my fax line at 818 706 8540, or over my secured confidential phone line and phone service at 818 706 8458.
Send checks to:
Dr Joshua David Stone
Melchizedek Synthesis Light Academy
28951 Malibu Rancho Rd., Agoura Hills, CA 91301

Please also check out all the New Services of the Melchizedek Synthesis Light Academy on my Website. There is literally a Spiritual Goldmine of Services, Books, Articles, Meditations, and a Spiritual Museum in the "Image Gallery," which will be one of the most beautiful Spiritual Museums you have ever experienced, all in the comfort of your own home.

RECENT UNSOLICITED TESTIMONIALS ABOUT MY RECENTLY WRITTEN BOOKS ARRIVED BY EMAIL. SOME OF THESE WERE SO TOUCHING I FELT GUIDED TO SHARE THEM WITH YOU HERE:

Dear Dr. Stone,

I don't want to take up your time with a long e-mail so I will make it short. I am about halfway through *The Golden Book of Melchizedek* and I have never experienced this phenomenon from a book before, the book is literally giving off a spiritual light and energy. I don't know if it is how the book is phrased or written, but I have literally been in physical ecstasy since opening it. It is like an intense light shower. I don't know if your other readers will notice this or not but the book must REALLY be blessed for I have read several thousand books over the last 10 years and none of them have done this. Just wanted to alert you to the fact. It would be interesting to hear how and if other readers have experienced the same thing.

Sincerely,

Dear Dr. Stone,

I have finished both of your two new books, *The Golden Book of Melchizedek* and *How to Release Fear-Based Thinking*. They have helped me to completely transform my consciousness and attitude towards life. I am now open to receiving where before I was in a closed state of consciousness. If one reads and heeds these books and the techniques and ascension activations, one will go far quickly on the spiritual path. Ever since I read *The Golden Book of Melchizedek* I have been buzzing with bliss. That is something for one who usually suffers from clinical depression. There is more to these books than just paper and ink. The power and wisdom of the Universe are contained within and literally shower one with light and higher vibrations of the spiritual plane. *How to Release Fear-Based Thinking* helps to remove fear/negative ego and replace it with unconditional love. The results are a complete transformation of one's consciousness level and the resulting bliss will make one feel like "A million bucks." I haven't felt this good consistently in 20 years and I believe the change is permanent. Thank You and God Bless you Dr. Stone for authoring these life-changing books. I recommend that all Lightworkers and those just entering the spiritual path read and utilize these books as there are none finer you will find on your spiritual journey.

Sincerely,

Dear Joshua,

This book *How to Release Fear Based Thinking and Feeling: An In-depth study of Spiritual Psychology* is so good that seeing it in print is blowing my mind. You put all your heart, soul, mind and might into it and I am determined to finish it before I dare read the *Golden Book of Melchizedek!*

Sincerely,

Dear Joshua,

I received you new book *How to Release Fear-Based Thinking and Feeling: An In-depth Study of Spiritual Psychology* just before Christmas and it was a most wonderful Christmas present! Already I am 100 pages into it and finding it absolutely superb and extremely illuminating!

Sincerely,

Dear Dr Stone,

Thanks for your email! It's great to hear from you again! Since I wrote to you, I'm now about 250 pages into *How to Release Fear-based*

Thinking and am savoring every page!! I've found it extremely insight-ful and invaluable. Along with *Soul Psychology*, I've been using various tools, which have had an enormous affect on me. I'm nearly finished using your 21-day program for removing negative habits, which I have used for removing all fear programming of attachment and feelings of loneliness. Even after a week, I felt a tremendous difference!

My life circumstances were making me feel pretty lonely and iso-lated, only now I've learned that I am the only one that makes my feelings and not circumstances or other people! I also seem to have a much greater ability to push out my negative ego and whenever I feel it starting to rear its ugly head I zap it out. It's amazing that with practice you become more and more aware of whether you are thinking from an ego or a Spiritual perspective. I really must thank you, because these changes, which are a direct result of reading your books and applying their techniques, have had such a hugely benefi-cial effect on me.

Sincerely,

Joshua,

I got the *How to Release Fear-Based Thinking* book on Saturday and began reading it immediately. That book is truly inspired! I never found my Big Questions answered or even addressed in the field of traditional psychology, so your book is like a Godsend to me. I feel like I've waited a long time for a book like this!

I'm only on chapter five and there's so much more to take in. I really feel a supportive energy coming out of the book into my aura while I'm reading it: The energy that flows out is a combination of love, wisdom and power; it is the three-fold flame that you speak of in the book that seems to permeate the book's aura, and your aura while you wrote it. And much more than that. I find myself going into altered states while reading the book, and sometimes feeling close to tears while having huge realizations in the process of reading it. And all this in the first 50 pages or so. My gratitude is beyond words.

I am really moving through your book! Your observations and corrections on channelings are most valuable! I can see more clearly now where my own channelings are faulty, being mental rather than spiritual at times. There are so many good things in this book, by the time I finish I'll have another great testimonial to give you.

One thing I totally love about your book is your honesty! You're bringing some much-needed corrections to many of us who've been non-discerning with New Age books and channeled materials.

Sincerely,

Dear Joshua,

Finished reading but never finished. All your books are great but this one, *How to Release Fear-Based Thinking and Feeling* is a DIAMOND! Thanks for awakening me from a nightmare that I thought was real! Now I must review all I've read so the real work can begin anew! I catch myself doing or saying something wrong every day so how do I have time to see someone else's log when my own is blinding!

Sincerely

Dear Dr Stone:

I have so much I would like to share with you regarding the *How to Release Fear-Based Thinking and Feeling* book, that I don't know where to begin.

This is the book I've been waiting for all my life, and now I've found it. You are so comprehensive in your observations of how the negative ego has corrupted our thinking that I've finally freed myself and shed a few hundred pounds of negative ego that had seeped into my belief system. It's amazing how tricky the negative ego is and how it justifies itself to you so that you'll keep believing in it, giving it life. I can see now how it has no reality outside our corrupted world of thought. And I can see how the only real way to think is Christ/Buddha thinking. Your book is totally changing my life, and after few weeks of careful study, I would say this is the best book I've read in my life! And that is a lot to say because I have read a ton. This is the answer to my prayers. I'm getting so much from this book that I'm able to clearly see myself teaching these principles to others, through counseling sessions and with small groups.

Sincerely

Beloved Joshua:

I am now on page 144 of the *Full Spectrum Prism Synthesis Bible* book, and was forced to stop right here, focusing on your last paragraph on the page, to express my gratitude.

Thank you for teaching me how to acquire inner peace after riding on an emotional rollercoaster most of this lifetime, never knowing how to save myself from drowning. Now I am able to live in the center of any cyclone, no matter the speed of the wind or the roar of the turbulent sea.

Gratefully,

Dear Dr Stone,

I want to express my deepest gratitude for your new manuscript books publication. They literally opened my eyes wide to the comprehension of the "integration and balance" of Ascension issues. I am one-quarter way through in completing reading the book called The Golden Book of Melchizedek and it is indeed magnificent and a seven-star rating!

Sincerely,

Dear Dr. Stone,

Your book *How to Release Fear-Based Thinking and Feeling* is a great book. You are right, everyone should read this book. It is like a finely tuned and oiled machine. It is a course within itself. I see now why the Masters wanted you to make it available ahead of schedule. Good Job!

Love,

Dear Dr. Stone,

I purchased your manuscript *The Soul's Perspective on How to Achieve Perfect Radiant Health*. Extraordinary book!

With Love and Light,

Dear Dr. Stone,

Hi again! You may remember speaking to me a month or so back (most people have a hard time trying to forget me!). First of all, since last speaking to you I have now finished reading *How to Release Fear-Based Thinking and Feeling*. WOW!!! As I said before, it has had a profound impact on me in many ways. You mentioned that each chapter was like a "chiropractic" adjustment. Well, I was aware of these adjustments and shifts even before you talked about them! I don't think I've quite experienced anything like it before. I could feel old programming and old belief patterns gently shifting and transforming. Anyway, the book, along with your other books, has helped me so much in every area of my life. They have truly helped me weather the storm and, indeed, dispel the storm! All I can say is a heart-felt thank you.

Sincerely,

Dearest Joshua,

I have just finished reading the Golden Book and must say it is the most comprehensive of all your wonderful books on tools and meditations for integrated ascension.

Sincerely,

* *

17

"Is There Such a Thing as Positive Anger?"

Dear Dr. Stone,

I am profoundly impressed by your book, *How to Release Fear-Based Thinking and Feeling.* I have read up to page 100 at this moment, and found it to be very thorough with one exception for which I would like your explanation.

In reading your favorite affirmations in chapter 13, I was totally taken aback when you referred to "positive" anger and a few lines later you say, "I am mad as hell." As you are so fond of saying, "I humbly submit that neither of these have any place in spiritual growth."

Being "mad as hell" or angry to me stem from fear-based thinking. Anger is a derivative of fear. Fear is a derivative of separative thinking or the ego, so how can it be positive except that we slip and make a mistake by allowing anger to form and then realizing what we are doing and stopping it and being determined not to do it again. Then replacing the anger with love or a derivative thereof.

To me anger is a loss of peace and a falling into limitation; believing that someone or something outside of us is more powerful than we and causing us problems or we get angry with ourselves because we find ourselves guilty of some wrong act—we see ourselves as sinners. Thus, anger at ourselves prohibits us from gaining any wisdom from the resolution of our mistakes. You may explain what you mean by positive anger later in the book, if so I apologize for this letter, but just so it does not bug me, I would appreciate your explanation. I know another master who gets angry with her students. She also claims that it is positive, that she is angry or showing anger for her students' benefit. But I still find it hard to swallow. As I see it, a display of anger, for whatever purpose, is still a display of anger or a loss of self-control. I hope you can enlighten me on this subject.

Thanks again for all your hard work.

Much Love,

Dr. Stone's Reply:

Greetings my friend!

Thanks for your email and kind words. They are much appreciated. Thank you as well, my friend, for your question. There are a number of lenses and lessons here so let me explain!

The first lesson is always to read the whole book before you make any conclusions, for you will find I teach 100% exactly what you said. Anger is negative ego, so I agree with you and that is what the entire book says. Even read the chapter on anger I wrote and I tell how to get rid of it completely 100% by just changing your thinking. Anger stems from attachment, not protecting one self, and not looking at things as lessons and Spiritual tests. This woman you spoke about who takes her anger out on people is doing nothing more than indulging her negative ego mind and nothing more and this is exactly what every word in this book teaches, if you read the entire book!

The only reason I left that particular affirmation in was that was taken from the channelings of the Universal Mind through Edgar Cayce. I have a lot of respect for those channelings, and this was a term the Universal Mind used. It is a term that might be useful to some very young souls who are trying to transform anger into personal power. Peace Pilgrim spoke of this as well. The idea being to use the power in anger, if caused by the negative ego, and channel it into Personal Power and unconditional love. So that was all I was really thinking in leaving it in. For the record books, it is not an affirmation or a concept I find useful personally, however, for some souls who work with the Edgar Cayce material or are younger souls I left it in.

There is also the concept of the Spiritual Warrior. A great many light-workers focus on Love but are so lacking in personal power and mastery it is mind blowing. They are spaced out, scattered, dingy, and much more, which I say with no judgment. Without owning one's 100% personal power, it is impossible to control your thoughts, feelings, emotions, and be unconditionally loving. Master Kuthumi has spoken quite extensively on the value of such a concept and he is the World Teacher or one of them. Owning one's personal power for most people is a very difficult thing, as you know. So I was fudging a little bit leaving that affirmation in to allow people who are still stuck in a personality level understanding. The mark of a good teacher is to be able to speak to all levels—beginning, intermediate, and advance.

You are more advanced, my friend, and I honor you for this and it is a breath of fresh air to hear your views about anger for what you said is word for word what I believe and if you read the rest of the book you will find no place in the book where I say anger is appropriate. Every word in the book teaches exactly the opposite. Part of being a good Spiritual teacher is also the ability to teach from a Full Spectrum Prism Consciousness perspective, which means from many lenses. Personal power is so hard a thing to teach people I was using a personality level concept to teach a Spiritual lesson. The same applies to how I dealt with grief. Grief, in truth, is negative ego in the highest Spiritual Ideal. This is also a hard pill for people to understand and swallow who come from the personality level psychology which almost all do, including most Spiritual Leaders and teachers. So I was just fudging, my friend, to try and bridge personality level psychology and true Spiritual psychology.

I left in the other one about "I am as mad as hell and I am not going to take it anymore" because of the movie *Network*, which won Best Picture of the year at the time I wrote most of those affirmations! People were fascinated with that scene in the movie with Peter Finch, and again I was fudging at the time to help people channel their anger into personal power. All the teachings in all my books 100% clearly state that anger is negative ego. I am one of the few Spiritual Teachers who has come out 100% clearly to say all negative feeling and emotions are 100% negative ego, period. So, my good friend, you are jumping to conclusions a little bit, however, I do understand.

The last thing I will say on this point is, I very humbly tell you that I have been given an enormous amount of Spiritual Leadership and responsibility by the inner plane Ascended Masters. I am attaching an article to this letter that will more deeply explain my Spiritual Mission. I share this only to say that putting on Event like Wesak for

2000 and writing a 40 volume Ascension Book Series, running an Academy, answering every email, lecturing, teaching, and everything else I do takes an enormous amount of time. That list of affirmations was written almost 20 years ago when I wrote the first version of *Soul Psychology*. I have written 30 new books since then. As a service to my readers, I added those affirmations from this book. Since this book was written 20 years ago and edited already, I did not see the need to read the chapter again. They served a purpose 20 years ago for the reasons I mentioned above. However, I live in such a transcendent reality myself where I don't even use a concept like Spiritual Warrior for I don't need it myself. 20 years ago it was useful to me and still remains useful to a great many people which is why Master Kuthumi speaks of it so much, however, once one truly becomes a master of their energies certain personality bridging concepts are no longer needed. At that time 20 years ago they were useful to me and the work I was doing. They are not anymore and you will find absolutely not a single word in this book or any of my other books that teaches anger being a good thing. It is 100% negative ego!

As a matter of fact I tell a very cute story teaching this lesson to my students where over 25 years I was angry about something and I was journal writing to my Higher Self and I said I am not going to let go of this anger until this situation resolves itself. That night I dreamed God died! You have never seen anyone in the infinite universe let go of anger so quickly in your entire life. This was 25 years ago. So if you think I believe in anger, nothing in this infinite universe could be more opposite. I was just quoting the Universal Mind though Edgar Cayce. I was trying to give an assortment of affirmations that people from all paths and walks of life could use. Even at that time I didn't use that one myself personally for I didn't believe in anger and I even

100% clearly stated anger was 100% negative ego in my book *Soul Psychology* 20 years ago!

So, my friend, you are sharing this with one of the few Spiritual Teachers on Earth who also teaches Spiritual Psychology and is one of the biggest busters of personality level psychology on the planet. Keep reading and you will see!

So in closing, please forgive me for not taking those affirmations out. Again I say, they were concepts that were useful in my first edition of *Soul Psychology* 20 years ago because of the reasons I mentioned, however, this book is a 100% transcendent book, and in my opinion is the most advanced book on Spiritual Psychology on the market today. So to get 700 pages of the finest Spiritual Psychology teachings on this planet and have only these two personality bridges left in, I think you would agree, was still excellent. I am sure you understand my friend!

In closing, I congratulate you on your ability to see anger for what it truly is. I would estimate that 98% of all lightworkers are confused on some level on this point. You and I, my friend, are two of the few that are not! Thank you for the breeze of fresh air in this regard, for I am the one has been battling lightworkers in a totally loving way for 20 years on this point and in regard to all negative feelings and emotions! It is good to have some help! I welcome it!

I am your Eternal Spiritual Brother and Friend!
Adonai in the Light and Love of God and the Masters!
Dr Joshua David Stone

* *

18

On Huna Prayers and Manifesting

Hi Dr. Stone,

At the Wesak you stated that your grand success in attracting so many people to the Wesak was mostly because of your use of the Huna prayer and recommended that we use it.

Because of your high praise, I'm adapting that prayer for my endeavors. As I do so, old limiting beliefs are arising in me. It's interesting and very useful for me, as a psychologist myself, to be so confronted. Although I am very careful to include "clauses" like "if it is the will of God and in harmony with the divine plan...," I still balk at generating wealth while working on "spiritual" projects.

I have found a worthy project that I believe is in harmony with the Divine Plan. This project can be very lucrative to those who involve themselves with it. I've adapted the Huna prayer to include a few more of my favorite Gods and Goddesses plus address the success of our project at least in America and Canada so far, an attainable reality. However, my programming is bringing up doubts as to whether it is appropriate to ask God and the Hierarchy for assistance in a project that, however worthy, could make us very wealthy. Do you have any comments, advice, guidance, ritual, or principle to clear this matter, this area of my life?

Thanks,

Dr. Stone's Reply:

Greetings my friend!

I would say that the Huna prayers are a part of the reason for the success, not all. Each level of mind must do its part. Superconscious, conscious, and subconscious! The integration is the key. Only mastering one level will manifest nothing!

As to your question about praying for a worthy cause that makes money. This is some faulty programming from past lives and/or this one. It is perfectly fine to ask the Masters for help on this level. God is a part of the Material Plane as well! Think of it this way: the more money you make the more you can give away to help other people. This is how I think about it and what I do. It is always good, however, to examine your motives to make sure your intentions are truly Christed and not coming from the negative ego. As long as this is the case and there is no delusion of the negative ego going on, then it is 100% fine and appropriate to ask God and the Masters for help!

God must be realized on all four levels: Spiritual, mental, emotional, and material! How will you fulfill your Spiritual Mission, puzzle piece, and Spiritual Contract on Earth if you have no money? Just do not be attached to money and do not make money

your God, as most people do. Make it a preference not an attachment! Hope this helps!

Warmest Regards,
Dr Joshua David Stone

* *

19

"I Need a Book on Spiritual and Emotional Quotients"

Dear Dr. Stone:

Please tell me where I can get information on Theories of Spiritual Quotient by Donah Zohar, Emotional Quotient by Daniel Golman, IQ as per your article, Yoga Helps Leverage Your Personality by R. Venkateshan.

Please tell me if there is any book on these topics by Donah Zohar and other resources.

Regards,

Dr. Stone's Reply:

Greetings my friend!

There is only one book that I have ever seen that speaks of all the various quotients in an integrated manner on a Spiritual, psychological, and Physical/Earthly level; these are my books *Integrated Ascension: Revelation for the Next Millennium* and *The Golden Book of Melchizedek: How to Become an Integrated Christ/Buddha in this Lifetime*! You will find how to order these books on my Website: http://www.drjoshuadavidstone.com

Sincerely,
Dr Joshua David Stone

✳ ✳

20

"Is There a Course to Develop Psychic and Intuitive Feelings?"

Dear Dr. Stone:

I want to know are there any courses—correspondence, full-time for developing and understanding psychic/intuitive feelings. I keep on having these intuitions about people that I know and I want to enhance it further by understanding it better. Please let me know if there are any associations in India or abroad who do this. I would really appreciate it if you could provide me with the addresses and e-mail.

Thanks.

Dr. Stone's Reply:

Greetings my friend!

Yes, the Melchizedek Synthesis Light Academy has set up a type of correspondence course for people all over the world. By studying my

31 books on Spiritual, Psychological, Psychic, and Earthly Growth, working with my 13 audio Ascension Activation Meditation Tapes, and learning to transcend negative ego thinking and programming, your Spiritual and Psychic gifts will be greatly sharpened and increased, my friend! It is for this reason these books, tapes, and my Website have been created so that people all around the world can tap into it and take advantage of it in the comfort of their own home!

Warmest regards,
Dr Joshua David Stone

* *

21

"I Get Easily Depressed"

Dear Dr. Stone:

I get easily depressed/distressed by small setbacks and unpleasant encounters with people. I do my best to avoid such people, though it plays on my mind.

Sincerely,

Dr. Stone's Reply:

Greetings my Friend!

You said the key word, it plays on you "mind"! You must realize that your thoughts create your reality. All feelings are created by the mind, not by anything outside of self. You get depressed and distressed because you interpret life from the negative ego mind instead of your Spiritual/Christ/Buddha mind. Depression is caused by not owning your personal power and having a Spiritual Warrior attitude and by living too much out of the emotional body. Everything in life is a

Spiritual Test to see if you can respond from your Christ/Buddha mind. This is not your fault, you just need training. That is why Spirit has guided you to me. Read my books *Soul Psychology* and *How to Release Fear-Based Thinking and Feeling: An In-depth Study of Spiritual Psychology.* You will find them on my Website: http://www.drjoshua-davidstone.com

This will give you all the training you need to have inner peace at all times! Trust my guidance and you will be healed! You just need a little training, that is all! This should be taught in school, however, unfortunately it is not!

Warmest Regards,
Dr Joshua David Stone

✳ ✳

22

"It is Hard to Escape the Dual Mind"

Dear Dr. Stone:

Why does it sometimes seem so hard to escape from the dual mind? Do negative thoughts and feelings make part of duality necessarily? Please, tell me an easy way to have objective and constant good thoughts, and how to achieve a universal mind focused not in the duality, but in what is beyond duality. What is beyond duality, the perfection of God? The music that takes place in every single seed and weed? Your simple words will help me to understand.

Hope everything is going fine.

Love,

Dr. Stone's Reply:

Greetings my friend!

Transcending duality really means transcending the negative ego mind. There is always polarity of yin and yang even if negative ego did not exist. The negative ego creates negativity within polarity. Living within the polarity of third-dimensional experience can be a totally unconditionally loving and positive experience at all times. It is just the negative ego thoughts that make it not that way. To control the negative ego mind is not the easiest thing to do. If you study my books *Soul Psychology* and *How to Release Fear-Based Thinking and Feeling* they will teach you how to easily do this! These are the training manuals. So study them and it will be done!

Warmest regards,
Dr Joshua David Stone

* *

23

All Beings are Created by God

Greetings my friend!

Thanks for your emails! You will love the new books!

As to your email about this being, I consulted Spirit and the Ascended Masters and what they said is that what this being said was not accurate. It is a lesson in Spiritual discernment. All beings on Earth, or any other planet for that matter, no matter how they look are created by God and/or the Christ Consciousness or Holy Spirit. It is the choices we make as incarnated gods that determines our realization of God. However, clearly all are created by God, Christ, and the Holy Spirit. There is only one Son or one Daughter and we are all part of that same Sonship or Daughtership. Said another way, we all are the Eternal Self created by God!

Keep up the good work, my friend!

Much Love,
Dr Joshua David Stone

* *

24

"Can You Help Me Interpret This Dream, Dr. Stone?"

Dear Dr. Stone,

How are you doing? I had an interesting dream last night and I believe this is important as I am going through some Spiritual Tests now. There are very few dreams that I know are giving me some messages. I would appreciate you spending a few moments of your precious time.

Thank you so much.

Dream:

One fine day, when I could take the worldly life no more, I decided to go live in the forest where I knew some people had gone before and they had an ashram. I had just started my journey when I happened to meet a friend and told him about my plans. He advised to take some money; that it would be helpful initially. I remember taking about $145. I took *a few steps forward and I met two people who were staring at me as if analyzing me. The first person stared at me and passed by, but the second person continued to stare at me for quite some time. There was something different about this person. His eyes were dark; at least one eye was covered with dark glass. I was not afraid and so I stared back into his piercing eyes. Then a third person came to me and said, "Since you have decided to come to us, you need not take any money with you." I happened to find another friend passing by and I gave him the money and followed these three people. It occurred to me that these three people were there to be observers.*

As I reached the ashram, I was surprised to see so many people. There people of all kinds, old and young children together, however, there were two major parties and an election was in progress. I remember somebody telling me that the two parties are like "rain" and "hot sun." I intuitively felt "rain" was better than "hot sun." As I went in to the open, it was a beautiful pleasant day with a nice landscape. There was plenty of greenery and open places for all kinds of games. I saw people playing with large balls, some playing basketball. I started to play with a ball, but then something else caught my attention. I saw some people planning to do high jumps, but they were afraid. I knew I was an expert at high jumps and I had done well with that earlier in life. So I approached the target and decided to jump. There were a couple of obstacles in my path to the jump, which I cleared and then I ran toward the bar to jump. Deep in my heart I knew this was an easy jump, however, there was also a slight fear of 1 to 2 percent.

I woke up at this time and knew I had to document this in my dream journal.

Dr. Stone's Reply:

Greetings my friend!

Thanks for your email. As you know, every part of a dream is part of you and is symbolic of an aspect of self. Your dream is showing a letting go of the materialistic side of life to focus on the Spiritual. The forest is symbolic of these more Spiritual energies. You most focus on being integrated. Aspects of you at this time are in a state of observation watching yourself in an introspective manner and watching your path, which is good. Dark glass over one eye means a little work on clearing your perspective to a lighter perspective is needed, although, overall the dream is clearly very positive. Rain and hot sun are kind of like the yin and yang. You gravitate toward the Goddess path. High jumps are symbolic of Spiritual leaps you are making in your life. The last jump you did well, but the dream is showing a little bit of fear, which is just negative ego trying to get in. You were successful, this shows Mastery and shows just a small bit of Mastery needed to completely rid self of negative ego thoughts. In conclusion, I would say this is a very positive dream showing that you are moving in an excellent direction. Polish up those small spots, however, overall, Spirit is saying you are doing well!

Warmest Regards,
Dr Joshua David Stone

* *

25

"Earthly Life is Tough, This is a Fact!"

Dear Dr. Stone:

I have just received your books!!! On what has been a very interesting day—my checking account was closed this morning and even though it is the bank's mistake they won't reopen it, even when I went down there and it shows up on their computer that it is their mistake, they still wont reopen it!

Then there is the problem that I am having with the investor who financed my car and is harassing me. This resurfaced with him demanding that I return the car by today, this is totally out of alignment with our contract!

And finally, I have been staying with my brother for the past week and he asked me to leave because my laughing bothers him!!!

With the investor and my brother, I have been very loving and supportive. I financed my brother's college and paid his rent and bills for years. I am reading your books, but I really do feel that I am under some sort of attack!!!

Also, I had a great meeting with an investor this weekend and he was going to give me $200,000, then he said my project made a bigger impact than he wanted!

I am leaving today to get an MRI at the hospital, and I honestly do not know where I am going; with nowhere to stay, a car that might not be mine in a few days, and no funding. I am laughing it is sooo crazy. Ooops! Better not laugh too much, that gets me into trouble.

Inside I feel calm and clear, like an observer, but I am exhausted from all of this.

I feel like going into the mountains, reading, and fasting for 21 days to clear this up.

Much love and deep appreciation.

You are a blessing.

Dr. Stone's Reply:

Greetings!

Earthly life is tough. That is a fact! There are also a lot of dark force energies worldwide and this is a time of great Spiritual Testing for everyone! The Master Jesus said, "Be ye faithful unto death and I will give thee a crown of life"! You must look at what is going on as a

Spiritual Test. It is a type of Job Initiation. I went through it in my life and everyone goes through it at sometime on the Spiritual Path. It is where everything is stripped away. Job "lost it" at first as well! However, then Job said:

Naked I come from my mother's womb and
Naked shall I leave!
The Lord giveth and the Lord taketh away,
Blessed be the name of the Lord!

This is what you need to say, my friend!

You also must say constantly: *Not my will, but thine, Oh Lord. Thank you for the lesson!*

As Sai Baba has said, "Welcome adversity." It will strengthen you if you deal with it with the proper attitude! Attitude is the key! Everyone can believe in God and have faith when things are going well. When the Spiritual Tests come that is the true test! It is good all is being stripped away, for all that is left is God, and you know who your true friends are!

Own you personal power as you have never owned it before. Become the Supreme Spiritual Warrior! Pray constantly to God, Christ, the Holy Spirit, the Archangels and Angels, and the Masters and Saints of your choice! As Edgar Cayce said, "Why worry when you can pray?"

Open a new bank account at another bank. You can get new checks in five minutes. If you get down to the point that you don't have money for food, let me know and I will send you some money! Just email me your address! No time for false pride! You would help me if the situation was reversed and you will help many others when the tide turns!

Attitude and prayer are the keys, and taking action in the physical world wherever you need to. Your power and mind, and God and the Masters' power, is an unbeatable team! Own your Personal Power 100% while simultaneously surrendering your life completely to God!

Constantly chant the name of God! Make a battleplan of everything you need to do on every level as to how to pass this Spiritual Test. Keep studying and reading.

Read this letter over every day as a Spiritual Attunement and Affirmation!

The Force is with you, my sweet friend, and Spirit and the Masters stand at your side.

Your morning pep talk!

Your Eternal Spiritual Brother and Friend!
Adonai in the Light and Love of God and the Masters,
Dr Joshua David Stone

* *

26

"I Met this Guy and Now it is Over, Any Advice?"

Dear Dr. Stone:

I need your advice, dear wise one. I was just talking with a dear friend of mine who is a healer and has a vibration very similar to yours, very pure and gifted and humble and a visionary and has GREAT TASTE IN FRIENDS...(me)—just kidding.

Anyway, this is my story and question. Remember that guy? Well, we have a very powerful connection and had a beautiful week together and were deeply in love. Everything was truly amazing and spiritual. Anyway, I came back here for two weeks to do the Internet projects and this guy was getting a loan for me to move out to be with him, and his mother loved me and she said she had dreams of me and that I was the woman her son was going to marry, etc. Then the bottom dropped out. I received an email that my age is an issue (I am older than him...don't look it a bit). He was the one who approached me and I had reservations about dating someone younger, but our experience of being together was amazing. He seemed older than me in a lot of ways and he convinced me that I could trust him that we were meant to be. Anyway, we broke up rather suddenly a few nights ago. I had it down to fear of intimacy and the fact that I am more spiritually aware than he is and all of that.

What my friend says is happening on a global level is that a lot of astral activity/interference is going on, and since this friend knows my history with men (the three really powerful relationships that I have had) all ended with this very abrupt turn around. He says that I need to do a clearing for this guy, and for myself, though I feel fine.

So, Joshua, I need your advice. This guy is Jewish and he does not believe in protection, astral anything, etc. We are not even communicating at this point, though honestly I do feel that something did cause some confusion and misdirection.

This is the position I find myself in, my old paradigm is control, that I need this specific person and I will light candles, pray, cry, be desolate for his love—that is not where I am any more. I believe now that I probably need someone with more spiritual experiences in their life, someone that is already grounded into their reality so that I don't overwhelm them. And when the fear comes up, we can both work through it together.

I also do feel that I want to help this guy clear. I get no pleasure from watching these men go from brilliant and full of light to half-awake and confused. That happened with my other two relationships. I NEVER thought about protection or clearing, et .

So, what to do?

How is Wesak coming along???

Joshua, despite this I am doing really well.

Much love,

Dr. Stone's Reply:

Greetings my friend!

Thanks for your very sweet and loving letter!

I also want to say I am very proud of you how you are handling this situation. You are demonstrating great Spiritual and Psychological maturity. What this shows is that you are much more solid in your right relationship to self and right relationship to GOD, which most people have not been trained how to do or maintain, especially in situations where relationships come into play! So congratulations from the Masters and myself. It shows how your thinking has really improved and how you are much more solid in your Christ/Buddha mind and how much negative ego thinking and emotions you have let go of. This was the first real Spiritual Test, and you have passed it with flying colors!

That being said, let's now move to your next questions. In regard to this guy, I think your read on it is pretty accurate. If you think about it, with no judgement intended, it is very "petty" to consider age. This is a very third-dimensional consideration that no Spiritually Conscious person would consider if all the other factors were right. As you say, he may be a very good person but a little too third-dimensional for you. This is a Spiritual Test for him whether he can get beyond this. It is perfectly okay to pray without the conscious permission of the other person as long as it is worded in the proper way. The way to set it up properly is to address the prayer to God, Christ, the Holy Spirit, and the Masters and Angels who you want to do the clearing work. Then write out your prayer on a piece of paper asking for exactly what you want cleared and for help in creating an inner plane healing and help if it is God's Will that he let go of this faulty thinking! In my humble opinion, if he doesn't want to be together that, of course, is fine, but chronological age should not be the reason why. Now the truth is he may not be at a level of Spiritual and Psychological development to transcend such personality level consciousness, with no judgement intended. If this is the case, it really is better that you not be with him. It means you need a more Spiritually and psychologically mature individual.

When you do this Huna-type prayer for a clearing, the key point is to ask "if it is okay with his Higher Self"! You must include this state-ment in the beginning of the prayer. As long as you do this, it is per-fectly fine and acceptable to pray for another. Now, in truth, usually one million out of a million times the Higher Self says "yes!" However, on very rare occasions the Higher Self may say "no," how-ever, this is unlikely. The main point being that you did not violate anyone's free choice. This is a very good lesson to learn and it is good that you asked! Now this is really perfect, for if the relationship is meant to be he will receive the healing and the inner plane guidance, direction and healing, and if it is not meant to be then you will not receive a response. In your Huna-type prayer state you preference, for it is 100% okay for you to have super strong preferences, just not *attachments*. The fact that you are as emotionally stable and as happy as you are in yourself shows that you remained in preference and not total attachment. This is good, my friend! You have learned well! After doing the prayer, surrender it to GOD, and the Masters and Angels and let them do their Divine Handiwork. Hold a 100% Positive

Mental Attitude without being attached but maintaining your preference. Affirm you will be happy either way. The reason this must be done is your first responsibility is to your self and GOD and this means you must maintain your happiness. Putting your happiness in a man instead of your proper Christ/Buddha thinking is idol worship, also known as "faulty thinking"! You are in a good place even though this has gone on because you are demonstrating this under fire! This is the true Spiritual Test of a Master! Following this approach assures you of inner peace and happiness either way, and assures that what is meant to be will take place. Be Patient, have Faith, and Trust! Have your strong preference, however, surrender to GOD'S Will. If it does not work out then GOD and the Masters have someone even better in mind! If it does work out, praise God as well! Life is always Win/Win when approached from Christ/Buddha thinking!

This is the Dr Joshua David Stone prescription. Take it once a day for three straight days and e-mail me after the full prescription has been taken! How about that for a Doctor's Prescription! The Force is with you!

Much Love,
Dr Joshua David Stone

* *

27

"How Do I Manifest My Desires?"

Dear Dr Stone,

Having stumbled upon your Website, I found it to be most interesting, if not inspiring. Having read some of your literature, which a friend gave me (i.e. a brief excerpt on the Laws of Manifesting), I decided to try and locate more information about your work and discovered your Website. Having been involved with meditation in one form or another for 4 or 5 years now (on and off), I have been extremely frustrated as I have recently been experiencing a very quiet time in my business activities. I manufacture a health product that I supply mainly to members of the public, via my Website in particular. However, for almost two months now, I have found business to have slumped quite dramatically. Although I only started my business just one year ago, I found it has done relatively well up until April of this year. At the moment, it has been far less productive in terms of sales, etc.

I decided to email you to inquire as to whether you may have some advice that I may follow (whether it be a book of yours or whatever other tools you may suggest may assist me in my "quest" to "get back on track"). I have always believed one's thoughts create one's reality, yet at present, I have been floundering a bit with regard to not manifesting my desires, which amongst other things would include manifesting many clients, financial wealth, etc.

I would greatly appreciate your feedback in this regard as to what steps you feel would be appropriate with regard to manifesting my desires. I would like to mention that I am deeply committed to my business and am extremely passionate about what I do. Although money is not the motivating factor that drives me, it is nevertheless necessary as I am not "living on a mountaintop in Tibet".

I thank you for your time and look forward to your response at your earliest convenience.

Best Regards,

Dr. Stone's Reply:

Greetings my friend!

Thanks for your email! I am so glad you found some of my work and my Website! You have found Spiritual Gold, my friend, of a greater value than even you yet know!

Seek ye the Kingdom of God and all things shall be handed unto thee! I teach people the Laws that govern both Heaven and Earth, and this is true secret to being both Spiritually Wealthy and Wealthy in an Earthly sense, which contrary to popular understanding, is

God's wish for you as well! The more money you have the more you can use it to be of service to others!

I will tell you what you need to do to be Wealthy on all levels beyond your wildest dreams and expectations! Read and study my books *Soul Psychology*, *How to Release Fear-Based Thinking and Feeling*, *The Golden Book of Melchizedek: How to Become an Integrated Christ/Buddha in this Lifetime*, and *The Complete Ascension Manual*! I have written 31 books, but these are the books you should read!

Then get my 15 Ascension Activation Meditation Tapes and work with one tape a day every day, and on the Seventh Day rest! Study the Website! If possible come to the Wesak Celebration! If you follow this simple guidance you will not only learn the secrets of how to become Wealthy beyond your dreams, you will, more importantly, become God Realized, become an Ascended Master, Spiritual Master, Self Realized, Self Actualized, and be of service to your Brothers and Sisters in the Divine Plan! You will fulfill your Spiritual Mission for incarnating, fulfill your Spiritual Contract, your personal blueprint in the Divine Plan, and embody God on Earth. You will move into Spiritual Leadership and Planetary World Service in the way and form that God would have you do it and in a way that makes you tons of money! You are blocked because God is speaking to you in the only way that will get your attention! To your credit, you have listened and God and the Masters have guided you to me for Spiritual training! This you can do without ever leaving the comfort of your own home!

All the Books and Tapes can be ordered through the Website! You are about to go through the most profound Spiritual, Psychological, and Physical/Earthly Transformation of your entire life!

Warmest Regards,
Dr Joshua David Stone

＊ ＊

28

"What Is It that Causes Things to Happen?"

Dear Dr. Stone:

What is it that causes things to happen, things behind which I can't find a reason? Someone is born in a rich man's mansion while another life form is born a pauper, some one is just crushed to death all of a sudden, and somebody is just wiped out from the face of the earth! I do not want an answer relating to the last birth's karma and all, I want something more feasible.

Sincerely,

Dr. Stone's Reply:

Greetings my friend!

The answer to your question is the Law of Karma, Cause and Effect, What you Sow is what you Reap! All souls are created equally, however,

God gives each person free choice. All Creation is caused by thought! Thought causes feelings, emotions, behavior, energy, and all action! Everything is God! All is One! All is Interconnected! What you do to another is literally what you do to self, for all that exists is the Self! It appears as separate in third-dimensional reality, but this is illusion! So in terms of your question, you are seeing the reflection of each person's thought creation and this law does extend over past lives! Those who manifest from negative ego/fear-based/separative consciousness will have negative rebirths. Those who manifest from Spiritual/Christ/Buddha consciousness will have good karma. This is how the Universe works. People can change karma by positive thinking, kind words, good deeds, prayer, meditation, and service work!

For more information study my Website at: http://www.drjoshua-davidstone.com

Namaste!
Dr Joshua David Stone

* *

29

"Am I Attracting These Negative People?"

Dear Dr. Stone:

I LOVE the books…you are so gifted!

For me, almost everyone, especially those who decisions could have a major effect on my life, seem seduced by their negative ego. I see the seduction, almost feel it, and how they go for that without even thinking of the consequences.

I know that it is perspective and what is inside, etc. However, I have to be honest, I don't get the hit that I am the origin of a lot of this. I also get tested by my chiropractor daily for physical as well as emotional and psychological issues, and I keep coming up clear.

If I am delusional PLEASE TELL ME! I search for truth!

Again, you are in my prayers and in my heart.

Much love and appreciation,

Dr. Stone's Reply:

GREETINGS MY FRIEND!

THANKS FOR YOUR EMAIL. I AM FINE! JUST INCREDIBLY BUSY AFTER WESAK. IT IS THE BUSIEST TIME OF MY YEAR AND I AM PILED A MILE HIGH WITH WORK FROM ALL ANGLES AND LEVELS AND I AM SLOWLY BUT SURELY GETTING ON TOP OF IT!

IN TERMS OF YOUR QUESTION, THIS IS VERY IMPORTANT TO UNDERSTAND. I AM NOT SAYING THAT YOU ARE CAUSING ALL THE NEGATIVE EGO PEOPLE AROUND YOU, FOR NEGATIVE EGO PEOPLE ARE EVERYWHERE. NEGATIVE EGO PEOPLE CRUCIFIED JESUS. IT IS NOT ALWAYS PERSONAL TO YOU OR ANYONE ELSE. SO, DON'T PUT THAT TRIP ON YOURSELF. ALL I AM SAYING IS THAT YOU CAUSE AND CREATE HOW YOU REACT OR RESPOND TO PEOPLE. AS YOU MASTER WHAT I AM TEACHING YOU IN THIS BOOK, THESE PEOPLE WILL NOT KNOCK YOU OFF BALANCE SO EASILY. YOU WILL RETAIN YOUR CENTEREDNESS AND CALMNESS EVEN WHEN THEY DO THESE THINGS. YOU WILL ALSO LEARN TO CONTROL THE NEGATIVE EGO IN YOUR SELF MORE AND BE ABLE TO SEE IT MORE CLEARLY IN OTHERS SOONER. YOU WILL SEE THE RED FLAGS EARLY AND CONSCIOUSLY CHOOSE TO AVOID THESE PEOPLE. IF A PERSON CANNOT SEE THE NEGATIVE EGO IN SELF THEY CANNOT SEE IT IN OTHERS EITHER. NEGATIVE EGO PEOPLE WILL ALWAYS BE AROUND. YOUR

SPIRITUAL VISION TO SEE WHAT IS GOING ON AND HOW TO
DEAL WITH THEM WILL BE BETTER, WHICH MAKES ALL THE
DIFFERENCE IN THE WORLD!

MUCH LOVE,
DR JOSHUA DAVID STONE

* *

30

On the Corruption of Channeling

Greetings my friend!

Thanks for your emails. In regard to the book you are reading, with no judgment intended, I would recommend you stop reading. It is a corrupted teaching. This is not Jesus speaking, it is the contamination of the beliefs of an unclear channel! Don't clutter your mind with such negative ego corruption! You are learning a lesson about how the consciousness of a channel corrupts channeling! The New Age Movement is filled with this. Ninety-nine percent of all channelings you read will be corrupted by the consciousness, negative ego, beliefs, personal agendas, and unclarity of the person doing the channeling! An important lesson!

Much Love,
Dr Joshua David Stone

* *

31

"How Can I Channel?"

Dear Dr. Stone:

I am 59 years old and deeply interested in spirituality. Can I do channeling by myself? Please can you guide me on how I can get in touch with the Ancient Masters?

Dr. Stone's Reply:

Greetings my friend!

Thanks for your question! Yes, everyone can get in touch with the Ascended Masters; however, everyone will channel them in a different way. Some are clairaudient. Some will channel telepathically! Some intuitively! Some through energy and healing and some through a more heart and feeling focus! No one is better than another is! More like different flowers in a beautiful garden! To learn how to channel study my Website and my books *Soul Psychology* and *The Complete Ascension Manual*! To be a proper Channel, one must master one's self Spiritually and Psychologically, for if one is not psychologically clear and is run by the negative ego and personal agenda it will contaminate the channeling! You will find how to achieve these ends by studying my books! It can't be learned in a second, however, it can be learned through a little study and practice if one is given the proper information and tools which these books and Website supply! http://www.drjoshuadavidstone.com

Warmest Regards,
Dr Joshua David Stone

* *

32

"Why did God Create the Universe?"

Dear Dr. Stone:

Why, according to you, did God create this Universe?

Dr. Stone's Reply:

Greetings my friend!

Well, my friend, this is quite a question to start my morning! I will humbly attempt to answer your most profound question! God created the infinite universe as an act of Unconditional Love to give creative expression to His Infinite Mind! God also created the infinite universe to share His Love and His Joy. He created Sons and Daughters who he gave free choice and free will to who could create and expand His Kingdom! So, God created the Infinite Universe out of Love, Joy and the desire for creative expression of His Infinite Mind. God breathed out the infinite Universe and breathes it back in! This is the In-Breath and Out-Breath of Brahma!

A great many of His Sons and Daughters have separated themselves from God, not in truth but in their own minds, by misusing the free choice God gave them in thinking with their negative ego or fear-based mind. This is why Sai Baba has said the definition of God is, "God equals man minus ego"! God's idea was that we, as his Sons and Daughters, would evolve through matter and the 352 levels of God returning back to Source not only as Gods as we have been from the beginning, but as "Realized Gods"! Each person is the Eternal Self, in truth, however, the purpose of life is to "Realize this truth and embody this truth" and evolve back to Source! The Spiritual path is really very simple! If you want to be with God in Heaven then think, feel, speak and act like God on Earth in your every thought, word and deed!

So let it be Written! So let it be Done!

Warmest Regards,
Dr Joshua David Stone

✳ ✳

33

"How Do I Deal With My Partner Needing Their Space?"

Dear Dr. Stone:

I made a friendship with a girl. I used to visit her frequently with something to eat because she was ill nourished. She greeted me very nicely and said, "You and I are friends." But today she says her self-image is damaged because of my frequent visits. She asked to stop my calls. All of this happened overnight, I could not tolerate this and I went into depression and disbelief.

Please help me!

Dr. Stone's Reply:

Greetings my friend!

The lesson here, my friend, is first to honor your friend's request. If someone asks for their space one should not hold on but honor their request. The lesson God is trying to teach you, my good friend, is to develop more "self-love" and "Love for God"! In life things are meant to be or not meant to be. This is not a rejection! There are many fish in the sea. The lesson here is that you are allowing what is called the negative ego mind to be critical and to attack self. You must learn to love self and love God and be whole and complete Spiritually and Psychologically in self so if a preference in life doesn't occur, you are not destroyed and/or do not abuse self. The real lesson here has nothing to do with the girl, but your need to develop more mastery over your thoughts and feelings and the need to Spiritualize your thoughts and feelings! It is now time to get more completely on your Spiritual path and that is why you are guided by God to write me. Study all the free articles on my Website. If you can, read and study my book *Soul Psychology* which will teach you how to be right with self and right with God. Become right with self and right with God first and then relationships will work out much easier for you. My books and Website will teach you to do this! http://www.drjoshua-davidstone.com

God loves you and you must allow yourself to receive this and you must love yourself! You must learn to love your own inner self and inner child. You must learn to properly parent yourself. God is wanting you to learn these lessons first, then life will work out much better as well as all relationships!

Sincerely,
Dr Joshua David Stone

* *

34

"Is Spiritual Discernment the Same as Intelligence?"

Dear Dr. Stone:

I hope you are doing well my friend, and thank you for your offer to advise me on materials related to discernment. Please inform me if you find I lack discernment or spiritual discernment in the material I deliver to you. This request I find proper to communicate with people both in daily life and across the Web. So far, I have tried to remain gentle, honest, and reliable in order to prevent people from sending viruses to my computer due to anger or misunderstandings.

When I connected to the Internet three years ago I decided to remain gentle and honest to all I would contact on the Web. Therefore, I always try to explain when I feel I am in error or somebody has corrected me from making a mistake in an e-mail. I often try to investigate the source of the error, and the most common type relates to the use of some types of discernment.

Is spiritual discernment the same as intelligence?

Dr. Stone's Reply:

Greetings!

Spiritual Discernment and Spiritual Intelligence are similar but not exactly the same! From within and from other people, information is coming to you. It is your job to be able to Spiritually discern and discriminate as to what is of God and what is of the negative ego. What is Love and what is attack/fear. What is separative and what is based on oneness. What is truth and what is illusion. What is of God and what is of the dark forces. What is negatively selfish and what serves everyone. What is ethical and moral, and what is self-serving! What is of the lower self and what is of the Higher Self! What is appropriate and what is inappropriate! With every thought you think, feel and act from, within and without, this must be Spiritual discerned so you are always thinking, feeling, speaking and acting God-like in everything you do!

Warmest Regards,
Dr Joshua David Stone

* *

35

A Letter to a Suicidal Person

GREETINGS MY FRIEND!

THIS IS DR JOSHUA DAVID STONE. I AM A PROFESSIONAL PSYCHOLOGIST AS WELL AS BEING A CHANNEL FOR THE MASTERS. WITH TOTAL UNCONDITIONAL LOVE AND COMPASSION IN MY HEART, I AM GOING TO GIVE IT TO YOU STRAIGHT. THIS COMES DIRECTLY FROM THE MASTERS AND FROM MY EXPERIENCE AS ONE OF THE LEADING SPIRITUAL PSYCHOLOGISTS ON PLANET EARTH. IN TOTAL HUMBLENESS AND HUMILITY, YOU ARE NOT GOING TO GET IT ANY CLEARER THAN THIS. YOUR LIFE IS ON THE LINE SO LISTEN CLOSELY!

THE MAIN REASON YOU FEEL YOU CAN'T DO WHAT SANANDA RECOMMENDED IS THAT ON A CONSCIOUS AND SUBCONSCIOUS LEVEL YOU HAVE "GIVEN UP"! YOU HAVE LOST YOUR WILL TO LIVE! THE WILL TO LIVE CAN BE EQUATED WITH THE WILL TO FIGHT—THE WILL TO BE A SPIRITUAL WARRIOR! THIS, IN PSYCHOLOGICAL TERMS,

COULD BE CALLED NOT OWNING YOUR PERSONAL POWER! YOU HAVE LOST YOUR PERSONAL POWER AND SELF-MAS- TERY OVER YOUR THOUGHTS AND FEELINGS. YOU HAVE BECOME A VICTIM, LETTING YOUR THOUGHTS AND FEEL- INGS RUN YOU, INSTEAD OF YOU RUNNING YOUR THOUGHTS AND FEELINGS. WHEN THIS HAPPENS, THE NEG- ATIVE EGO/FEAR-BASED/SEPARATIVE/LOWER-SELF MIND TAKES OVER. THE PURPOSE AND KEY TO A SUCCESSFUL LIFE IS TO THINK WITH YOUR SPIRITUAL/POSITIVE/CHRIST/BUD- DHA MIND. THIS IS BECAUSE, SWEET FRIEND, YOUR THOUGHTS CREATE YOUR REALITY! YOUR THOUGHTS CRE- ATE YOUR FEELINGS AND EMOTIONS. YOUR THOUGHTS CREATE YOUR BEHAVIOR.

BE CLEAR ABOUT THIS. THERE IS ABSOLUTELY NOTHING WRONG WITH YOU. WHAT THAT OTHER CHANNEL SAID TO YOU IS NOT TRUE. YOU ARE CHILD-LIKE, INNOCENT, HARM- LESS, AND GOOD EXACTLY AS YOU THINK YOU ARE. THAT CHANNELING WAS AN UNCLEAR CHANNELING. DO NOT GIVE YOUR POWER TO UNCLEAR PEOPLE. THE ONLY THING ARE SUFFERING FROM IS WHAT I CALL "FAULTY THINKING"! YOU ARE PERFECTLY FINE AND CAN CHANGE YOUR LIFE ANY TIME YOU WANT TO. YOUR PROBLEM IS NO ONE EVER TAUGHT YOU TO THINK PROPERLY! THIS IS NOT YOUR FAULT; IT IS A PROBLEM THAT MOST PEOPLE IN THIS WORLD HAVE. EVEN MOST SPIRITUAL PEOPLE AND PSYCHOLOGISTS DO NOT UNDERSTAND THIS. IN YOUR DARKEST HOUR, IN WHAT MIGHT BE CALLED THE DARK NIGHT OF YOUR SOUL, GOD HAS HEARD YOUR PRAYERS AND GUIDED YOU TO ME FOR TRAINING IN HOW TO THINK PROPERLY AND TURN YOUR LIFE AROUND! THIS IS ACTUALLY VERY EASY TO DO IF

YOU HAVE THE RIGHT TRAINING AND IF YOU ARE WILLING
TO MAKE A LITTLE EFFORT!

MY SUGGESTION IS TO NOT UNDERESTIMATE THE PRO-
FUNDITY OF THIS MOMENT AND THIS GRACE FROM GOD,
AND TO GIVE IT ONE MORE TRY. I ABSOLUTELY GUARANTEE
YOU THAT THIS PROGRAM WILL WORK. I HAVE HELPED
THOUSANDS OF SUICIDAL PEOPLE TO RETURN TO NORMAL
AND BECOME TOTALLY HAPPY AND HAVE INNER PEACE! AS
I SAID, IT IS NOT YOUR FAULT, IT IS JUST THAT NO ONE EVER
TRAINED YOU PROPERLY IN SPIRITUAL PSYCHOLOGY! IT
ONLY TAKES 21 DAYS TO CEMENT A NEW HABIT INTO THE
SUBCONSCIOUS MIND. IF YOU ARE WILLING TO MAKE AN
EFFORT AND MAKE ONE MORE TRY, I WILL SEND YOU ALL
THE BOOKS AND TAPES AND INSTRUCTIONS ON WHAT YOU
NEED TO DO, FOR FREE! YOU WILL NOT FIND A PSYCHOLO-
GIST OR PERSON ON PLANET EARTH WHO WOULD DO THIS
FOR YOU ANYWHERE ELSE, I HUMBLY TELL YOU. THE REA-
SON I AM DOING THIS IS THIS IS GOD HELPING YOU NOT
JUST ME! SO, GOD HAS HEARD THE PRAYERS OF PAIN OF
YOUR HEART AND SOUL AND GOD THROUGH ME AND WIS-
TANCIA ARE WILLING TO HELP YOU. ARE YOU GOING TO
TURN GOD DOWN? YOU HAVE FREE CHOICE AND YOU CAN!
GOD IS NOW OFFERING YOU A WAY OUT OF YOUR SELF-CRE-
ATED HELL. THE QUESTION IS, DO YOU HAVE THE EYES TO
SEE AND THE EARS TO HEAR THE PROFOUND GIFT YOU ARE
NOW BEING OFFERED? ALL YOU HAVE TO DO IS FOLLOW MY
INSTRUCTIONS!

GOD AND I REQUIRE ONLY ONE THING! THAT IS THAT YOU
BE WILLING TO MAKE AN EFFORT FOR ONE MONTH AS A
TYPE OF EXPERIMENT TO SEE IF WHAT I SAY IS TRUE AND IF

WHAT I SAY WORKS. I AM NOT SAYING IT IS GOING TO BE
TOTALLY EASY AND IT IS GOING TO TAKE SOME WORK ON
YOUR PART, HOWEVER, IF YOU FOLLOW MY SIMPLE
INSTRUCTIONS YOU WILL START FEELING A PROFOUND
TRANSFORMATION THE SECOND YOU START DOING WHAT
I SAY. THE NUMBER ONE THING YOU MUST DO TO BEGIN
THIS PROGRAM IS TO STOP THIS THOUGHT AND FEELING
OF GIVING UP AND PERSONALLY COMMIT TO TRYING THIS
PROGRAM FOR AT LEAST ONE MONTH. I ABSOLUTELY
GUARANTEE YOU THAT YOU WILL START EXPERIENCING
PROFOUND IMPROVEMENT! YOU WILL NEED TO READ THE
TWO BOOKS THAT I WILL SEND TO YOU FOR FREE, AND LIS-
TEN TO SOME TAPES THAT WILL GREATLY HELP!

IF YOU HOLD ON TO GIVING UP AND ARE NOT WILLING TO
TRY AND MAKE THIS PERSONAL COMMITMENT THEN THAT
IS YOUR CHOICE AND YOU WILL DIE! IN A SENSE, WHEN A
PERSON GIVES UP IN LIFE THEY ARE ALMOST ALREADY
DEAD! THE ONLY WAY TO BE SUCCESSFUL AND HAPPY IN
LIFE IS TO CLAIM YOUR PERSONAL POWER AND BECOME
MORE OF A SPIRITUAL WARRIOR, AND TO LEARN TO
BECOME A MASTER OF YOUR THOUGHTS AND FEELINGS
AND NOT A VICTIM OF THEM. YOU MUST LEARN TO PUSH
THE NEGATIVE EGO MIND OUT OF YOUR CONSCIOUSNESS
AND REPLACE IT WITH THE POSITIVE/SPIRITUAL MIND!
THIS IS WAY THE BIBLE SAYS, "LET THIS MIND BE IN YOU
THAT WAS IN CHRIST JESUS"! THERE ARE ONLY TWO MINDS
IN LIFE—A NEGATIVE EGO MIND AND A SPIRITUAL CHRIST
MIND. I WILL TEACH YOU TO THINK WITH YOUR SPIRI-
TUAL/POSITIVE CHRIST MIND, WHICH WILL HENCE CREATE
ONLY POSITIVE SPIRITUAL FEELINGS AND EMOTIONS! CON-
TRARY TO WHAT YOU CURRENTLY BELIEVE, IT IS YOUR

OWN NEGATIVE THINKING THAT IS CREATING HOW YOU FEEL, NOT ANYTHING OUTSIDE OF SELF!

IF YOU CHOOSE TO GIVE UP AND NOT TRY THERE IS NO JUDGMENT IN THIS, HOWEVER, YOU WILL FIND YOURSELF AFTER DEATH TOTALLY AWAKE AND ALIVE WITHOUT A PHYSICAL BODY, BUT IN THE SAME NEGATIVE MENTAL PLACE YOU ARE NOW! THEN YOU WILL HAVE TO BEGIN PLANNING TO REINCARNATE BACK TO EARTH OR ANOTHER PLANET LIKE EARTH TO DO IT ALL OVER AGAIN. WHAT I AM TELLING YOU IS AN ABSOLUTE FACT. SO, YOU CAN LEARN WHAT I HAVE TO TEACH YOU NOW OR YOU CAN LEARN IT NEXT LIFETIME AND KEEP REINCARNATING A MILLION MORE TIMES. THERE IS NO SUCH THING AS DEATH. EARTH IS A SCHOOL TO LEARN SELF-MASTERY. NO ONE HAS EVER TAUGHT YOU SELF-MASTERY. I WILL TEACH YOU SELF-MAS-TERY IN A VERY EASY TO UNDERSTAND MANNER THROUGH MY BOOKS AND LISTENING TO MY TAPES, WHICH I WILL GIVE YOU FOR FREE. YOU MAY ASK YOURSELF "WHY IS THIS MAN WHO KNOWS ME FROM ADAM, DOING THIS?" I AM DOING THIS BECAUSE GOD HAS ASKED ME TO! TO BE QUITE FRANK, I AM THE LAST TRUE CHANCE TO HEAL!

I AM WILLING TO HELP AND PUT YOU ON A PROGRAM TO RECOVER, BUT YOU HAVE TO BE WILLING TO SPIRITUALLY FIGHT AND SPIRITUALLY COMMIT TO GETTING ON A PRO-GRAM TO REMOVE ALL THE NEGATIVE THOUGHTS AND FEELINGS THAT ARE CURRENTLY IN YOUR CONSCIOUS AND SUBCONSCIOUS MINDS. I WILL SHOW YOU HOW TO DO THIS BUT YOU MUST MAKE THE EFFORT AND NOT GIVE UP FOR AT LEAST SIX WEEKS. YOU MUST BE WILLING TO MAKE ONE LAST ALL-OUT EFFORT FOR SIX WEEKS! I KNOW FOR

AN ABSOLUTE FACT THAT IF YOU MAKE THIS EFFORT IT WILL WORK! ARE YOU WILLING TO MAKE ONE LAST SUPREME EFFORT TO SEE IF YOU CAN BECOME A SPIRITUAL MASTER IN SIX WEEKS? THIS IS THE BEST OFFER YOU HAVE EVER GOTTEN THIS LIFETIME! THE QUESTION IS, "ARE YOU GOING TO LET YOUR NEGATIVE EGO MIND SABOTAGE YOU AND DESTROY YOU THIS LIFETIME AND NOT TAKE GOD'S OFFER?" I AM NOT EVEN CHARGING FOR MY TIME! THE ONLY THING I ASK IN RETURN IS THAT WHEN YOU RECOVER, YOU HELP SOMEONE ELSE AS I AND WISTANCIA HAVE HELPED YOU! YOU WILL NOT HAVE TO DO THIS UNTIL YOU FULLY RECOVER! I THINK THAT IS A FAIR DEAL. THAT YOU SELFLESSLY HELP SOMEONE ELSE IF MY TRAINING PROGRAM PULLS YOU OUT OF THIS! I THINK THAT IS A FAIR EXCHANGE! FIRST THINGS FIRST HOWEVER, AND LET'S GET YOU STRAIGHTENED OUT! IF YOU WOULD LIKE TO TAKE ME UP ON MY OFFER THEN EMAIL ME BACK AND I WILL TELL YOU WHAT NEEDS TO BE DONE!

IF, HOWEVER, YOU ARE NOT WILLING TO TRY AND MAKE AN EFFORT AND INSTEAD YOU CHOOSE TO INDULGE YOUR NEGATIVE EGO MIND AND FEEL SORRY FOR YOURSELF, THEN PLEASE DO NOT WASTE MY TIME, GOD'S TIME, OR YOUR TIME. I DO NOT MEAN THIS TO SOUND CRUEL OR UNCOMPASSIONATE. I AM JUST GIVING IT TO YOU STRAIGHT! I CAN 100% HELP YOU TO RECOVER, HOWEVER, AS THE SAYING GOES, "GOD HELPS THOSE WHO HELP THEMSELVES!" IF YOU ARE NOT WILLING TO MAKE AN EFFORT AND EVEN TRY TO RECOVER, THEN EVEN GOD AND THE MASTERS CANNOT HELP YOU! THE ABSOLUTE ONLY THING WRONG WITH YOU IS YOUR OWN NEGATIVE THINK-ING. OTHER THAN THAT, YOU ARE ACTUALLY PERFECT,

BELIEVE IT OR NOT! I WILL HELP YOU TO SEE THIS AND TOTALLY REPROGRAM YOUR CONSCIOUS AND SUBCONSCIOUS MINDS!

I END THIS LETTER WITH A QUOTE FROM THE *BHAGAVAD-GITA* WHERE ARJUNA GAVE UP MUCH LIKE YOU HAVE AND THIS IS WHAT KRISHNA SAID TO HIM AND WHAT I AM SAYING TO YOU RIGHT NOW! "GET UP AND GIVE UP YOUR UNMANLINESS AND GET UP AND FIGHT! THIS SELF-PITY AND SELF-INDULGENCE IS UNBECOMING OF THE GREAT SOUL YOU ARE"!

I WILL TRAIN YOU THROUGH MY BOOKS AND TAPES AND SOME INITIAL LETTERS HOW TO DO THIS! THE CHOICE IS YOURS! MEDITATE ON MY LETTER AND PRAY TO GOD IN YOUR OWN HEART AND MIND AND ASK GOD YOURSELF IF THE WORDS I SPEAK ARE THE TRUTH! YOU ALREADY KNOW! WHEN YOU HAVE 100% DECIDED IF YOU ARE GOING TO "LIVE OR DIE" AND WHETHER YOU ARE WILLING TO "SPIRITUALLY FIGHT OR GIVE UP," LET ME KNOW! I WILL HUMBLY ACCEPT WHATEVER YOU DECIDE! YOUR LIFE HAS COME DOWN TO THIS FINAL EXISTENTIAL MOMENT! THINK DEEPLY, FOR A LOT IS RIDING ON THIS DECISION! IS IT NOT WORTH SIX WEEKS OF YOUR LIFE TO SEE IF THIS WORKS?

WARMEST REGARDS,
DR JOSHUA DAVID STONE

* *

36

What Other People Think of Me is None of My Business

GREETINGS MY FRIEND!

THANKS FOR YOUR HONEST AND SINCERE LETTER! WHAT I HAVE TO SAY IS THAT "THIS GOES WITH THE TERRITORY." WHEN YOU STEP FORWARD IN SPIRITUAL LEADERSHIP AND MOVE TO THE FRONT LINES, YOU BECOME A TARGET FOR THE NEGATIVE EGOS OF OTHERS. MOST PEOPLE IN THE WORLD ARE RUN BY THE NEGATIVE EGO! MOST PEOPLE IN THE WORLD COMPARE, COMPETE, AND LIKE TO ATTACK AND CRITICIZE OTHERS BECAUSE THEY SUFFER FROM LACK OF PERSONAL POWER, SELF-LOVE, AND OVERALL CHRIST CONSCIOUSNESS. WHAT I HAVE TO SAY TO YOU IS LOOK AT WHAT JESUS HAD TO GO THROUGH 2000 YEARS AGO. LOOK AT THE CRUCIFIXION SAI BABA IS GOING THROUGH OVER THE INTERNET FROM THE NEGATIVE EGO AND DARK FORCES RUNNING SO-CALLED LIGHTWORKERS. ALL SPIRITUAL LEADERS HAVE TO DEAL WITH THIS. THESE ARE NOTHING MORE

THAN SPIRITUAL TESTS TO TEST YOUR POWER, LOVE, FAITH, CLARITY, AND INTEGRITY! IT IS TEACHING YOU TO NOT SEEK APPROVAL FROM OTHERS AND WORRY ABOUT WHAT OTHERS THINK. IF YOU ARE CLEAR IN WHAT YOU DO, THEN NO ATTACKS OR CRITICISMS OF OTHERS CAN STICK, FOR YOU KNOW YOU ARE IN INTEGRITY!

REMEMBER EACH MORNING TO PUT ON YOUR GOLDEN BUBBLE OF LIGHT SO OTHER PEOPLE'S NEGATIVE ENERGY SLIDES OFF YOU LIKE WATER OFF A DUCK'S BACK! EACH OBSTACLE THAT YOU OVERCOME JUST MAKES YOU STRONGER AND CLEARER. I SAY AGAIN, "IT GOES WITH THE TERRITORY"! THERE WAS A BOOK WRITTEN WITH A CUTE TITLE, "WHAT OTHER PEOPLE THINK OF YOU IS NONE OF YOUR BUSINESS"! STAY CENTERED AND STRONG IN YOUR CONVICTIONS AND IDEALS! AS THE MASTER JESUS SAID, "BE YE FAITHFUL UNTO DEATH AND I WILL GIVE THEE A CROWN OF LIFE"!

YOU SEE NOW WHY I HAVE WRITTEN SO MANY BOOKS TALKING ABOUT THE CORRUPTION OF THE NEGATIVE EGO! IT IS THE BLIND SPOT OF THE WORLD AND THE NEW AGE MOVEMENT! THIS IS WHY INTEGRATED ASCENSION IS SO IMPORTANT! DO NOT VEER FROM YOUR APPOINTED TASK! JUST AS IT IS IMPORTANT TO BE VIGILANT AGAINST ONE'S OWN NEGATIVE EGO, IT IS IMPORTANT TO BE VIGILANT TO NOT LET THE NEGATIVE EGO FROM OTHERS GET IN EITHER. PREPARE YOURSELF EACH MORNING BEFORE YOU START YOUR DAY! YOU ARE ON THE FRONT LINES NOW! YOU HAVE MY FULL SUPPORT! DO NOT LET OTHERS' NEGATIVE EGOS AND DARK FORCE ATTACKS CAUSE ANY LACK OF PERSONAL POWER, SELF-CONFIDENCE, AND FAITH IN SELF!

JUST MAKE A LIST ON A PIECE OF PAPER OF ALL THE REASONS WHY WHAT THEY SAY IS UNTRUE, AND THIS WILL CLEAR IT IF ANYTHING STARTS TO GET IT! HOLD FIRM TO YOUR OWN GOD THOUGHTS AND GOD CLARITY!

THE FORCE IS WITH YOU!

MUCH LOVE,
DR JOSHUA DAVID STONE

* *

37

"Was the Universe created to Give?"

Dear Dr. Stone:

Everything in Nature is constantly giving & giving…So the Universe was created to give…?

Dr. Stone's Reply:

Greetings my friend!

Interesting question, my friend. Yes, God or nature is constantly giving. It is the nature of life that once one becomes whole and complete within self to give and serve. Giving is the way we each as Sons and Daughters of God retain God for ourselves. For when we give, we receive! It is thought by some that giving is charity to others. In some cases this may be true, however, the greatest gift of giving is that which one receives one self. One cannot have God except by constantly giving God! It is by giving God that we retain God and receive God for ourselves. To give God we also must see God in all ways and all things. This is not to say that there is not a yin and yang in life and a time to give and receive. Part of being God is to learn to receive and integrate the Goddess or Yin aspect of life as well. So this question can be answered and seen from many lenses, my friend! Read more about the nature of God on my Website in all the free articles!

Warmest Regards,
Dr Joshua David Stone

* *

38

"When Will I Find Peace?"

Dear Dr. Stone:

I feel hopeless. I've lost the man I loved, I don't have a job, and I feel like committing suicide more often now. When will I find peace?

Dr. Stone's Reply:

Greetings my friend

This is a Spiritual test you are going through. What in the Western world and Bible is called the Job initiation! In truth, it is the best thing that ever happened to you and a blessing in disguise. However, you do not see this yet. This is why God has asked to speak to you in this moment through me, to bring you the inner peace you seek. So, listen closely!

This is a Spiritual test so that you will seek God first! Right now, you have attachments. As Lord Buddha said in his Four Noble Truths, "All suffering comes from Attachments"! "All suffering comes from wrong points of view"! You suffer not because of these outer things that are lost! You suffer because of your own negative thinking. You think with your negative ego mind instead of God's mind! In the Bible story, when Job had everything taken from him, he got depressed and wanted to die. Finally, he "woke up" and said, "Naked I come from my mother's womb and naked shall I leave! The Lord giveth and the Lord taketh away. Blessed be the name of the Lord"!

This is what you must say, my friend! This all is happening because your priorities are all confused. You do not put God first! You must learn to be right with self and right with God first in life and then seek these other things. The way to do this is to change your thinking. This is why Sai Baba has said, "God equals man minus ego"! You must learn to get rid of all the negative ego thoughts in your mind. Your thoughts create your feelings, not any outside thing. You must read my book *Soul Psychology* and *How to Release Fear-Based Thinking and Feeling* and study all the free articles on my Website, which will train you to think with your God/Krishna/Buddha/Atma/Eternal Self mind! I will train you how to reprogram your thinking, which will bring you inner peace, even starting today, although it will take 21 days to cement this new habit into your subconscious mind!

This is why you have written me. If you did not suffer like you did at first you would never have sought God! You would have never written me to get the answer from God. Don't you see the beauty of this? As the Bible says, "Seek ye the Kingdom of God and all things shall be added unto thee"!

You must learn to master your thoughts and feelings and emotions first, in service of God, and get on your Spiritual path and learn to think with your Spiritual mind, then you will have inner peace all the time and all the outer things will begin to manifest as well. This is the answer you seek! Now go and do your spiritual homework that God has given you!

Warmest regards,
Dr Joshua David Stone

* *

39

On the Job Initiation

Dear Dr. Stone:

I have been reading many of your articles and they have been a big help.

The last three years have been horrible for me, completely insane. I got into a situation that drove me to my knees. One man came against me so hard it was if he used an evil curse on me. I have been a Christian for years but God seemed to have left when all of these things happened. I lost my home, business, and the relationship I was in, and I still wait for God to mend things. Could I possibly ask your group to pray and ask God to restore my property and business, and the man I lost. It will have to be a miracle for things to turn around. Will you help?

Thank You

Dr. Stone's Reply:

GREETINGS MY FRIEND!

THANKS FOR YOUR EMAIL AND KIND WORDS. THEY ARE MUCH APPRECIATED! I AM SO PLEASED YOU ARE ENJOYING MY ARTICLES. YOU MUST READ SOME OF MY BOOKS. YOU WILL LOVE THEM! I HAVE NOW PUBLISHED 31 VOLUMES. ALSO DO CHECK OUT MY WEBSITE, FOR THERE ARE HUNDREDS OF FREE ARTICLES THERE AS WELL!

EVERYTHING YOU ARE GONG THROUGH IS A SPIRITUAL TEST. DO UNDERSTAND GOD NEVER LEFT YOU. WHAT HAPPENED IS THE NEGATIVE EGO MIND WAS INTERPRETING A LITTLE TOO MUCH OF YOUR REALITY. GOD HAS SENT YOU TO ME TO TRAIN YOU IN SPIRITUAL PSYCHOLOGY! GOD HAS HEARD YOUR PRAYERS, AND MY BOOKS, INFORMATION, WEBSITE, AND TAPES ARE GOD'S ANSWER! I WILL PRAY FOR YOU AND PUT YOU ON OUR ACADEMY INTERDIMENSIONAL PRAYER ALTAR!

WHAT YOU HAVE GONE THROUGH IS NOTHING MORE THAN THE JOB INITIATION AND THIS IS A GOOD THING, IN TRUTH, FOR WHEN EVERYTHING IS STRIPPED AWAY ALL THAT IS LEFT IS GOD! DID NOT JOB SAY "NAKED I COME FROM MY MOTHER'S WOMB, AND NAKED SHALL I LEAVE. THE LORD GIVETH AND THE LORD TAKETH AWAY. BLESSED BE THE NAME OF THE LORD"!

MARK MY WORDS, MY SWEET FRIEND, IF YOU FOLLOW THE GUIDANCE I AM ABOUT TO GIVE YOU YOU WILL RETAIN YOUR INNER PEACE AND ALL THAT YOU EVER WANTED IN AN OUTER SENSE, AND MORE. DOES NOT THE BIBLE SAY, "SEEK YE THE KINGDOM OF GOD AND ALL THINGS SHALL

BE ADDED UNTO THEE"! THIS IS TRUE BUT IT MUST BE DONE IN THE RIGHT WAY!

YOU HAVE NEEDED A SPIRITUAL TEACHER. WHEN THE PERSON IS READY THE TEACHER APPEARS. I WILL TEACH YOU THROUGH MY BOOKS, TAPES, AND WEBSITE! I DO THIS FOR MILLIONS OF PEOPLE ALL OVER THE WORLD AND THIS WORKS EVERY DAY! YOU ARE ALREADY SENSING THIS FROM THE ARTICLES.

HERE IS GOD'S GUIDANCE FOR YOU. YOU NEED TO ORDER AND READ TWO OF MY BOOKS TO START. THE FIRST BOOK IS CALLED *SOUL PSYCHOLOGY* THE SECOND IS CALLED *HOW TO RELEASE FEAR-BASED THINKING AND FEELING*! ORDER THEM FROM MY WEBSITE. THESE BOOKS WILL BRING YOU A PEACE THAT PASSETH UNDERSTANDING! DO NOT UNDERESTIMATE THE SIGNIFICANCE OF THIS MOMENT. YOU HAVE PRAYED AND GOD HAS HEARD YOUR PRAYERS AND HE IS ANSWERING THEM RIGHT NOW THROUGH ME.

ALSO GET A TAPE OF MINE CALLED "THE 18 POINT COSMIC CLEANSING MEDITATION"! YOU WILL ALSO FIND IT ON THE WEBSITE! LISTEN TO THIS MEDITATION TAPE EVERY DAY FOR 21 DAYS, ONCE A DAY!

FIND THE SECTION ON THE WEBSITE CALLED THE "INTERDIMENSIONAL PRAYER ALTAR PROGRAMS", READ ABOUT THEM, AND JOIN THE ONES YOU FEEL GUIDED TO JOIN! STUDY THE WEBSITE UNTIL YOU ORDER THE BOOKS AND THEY ARRIVE!

IN THE HOW TO RELEASE FEAR BOOK YOU WILL ORDER, WORK RIGHT AWAY WITH THE CHAPTER ON AFFIRMATIONS, THE CHAPTER ON HUNA PRAYERS, AND THE CHAPTER CALLED "THE CORE FEAR MATRIX REMOVAL PROGRAM"! READ THOSE CHAPTERS FIRST AND BEGIN PRACTICING THOSE TOOLS!

FOLLOW THIS SIMPLE GUIDANCE AND YOU WILL BE ON THE ROAD TO RECOVERY. TELL ALL YOUR FRIENDS ABOUT THE WORK!

WARMEST REGARDS,
DR JOSHUA DAVID STONE

* *

40

On the Use of Burning Pots

Dear Dr. Stone,

I'm happy to see that the Website and Wesak Festivals are flourishing. I started reading your books in 1995, and they have made a profound difference in my life.

I need your help!

In one of the books, you gave a "recipe" guaranteed to cleanse the energy in any room. I couldn't find it in any of my books. I am moving into a 30 year-old house and was wondering if you would please repeat the "recipe" for me? It had something to do with putting several things into a frying pan (alcohol, witch hazel?) and lighting it on fire.

I would be very grateful if you could send it to me. I have become a Buddhist nun and we are moving our meditation center into this older house. I would like to cleanse the energy before we start to fill it with our chants and prayers.

Thank you

Many Blessings,

Dr. Stone's Reply:

GREETINGS MY FRIEND!

THANKS FOR YOUR EMAIL AND SWEET NOTE! I AM SO PLEASED YOU ARE ENJOYING THE BOOKS! CAN YOU BELIEVE I HAVE COMPLETED 31 VOLUMES ALREADY! IF YOU LIKE THE EARLY BOOKS, WAIT UNTIL YOU SEE THE NEW ONES! YOU MUST READ MY TWO NEWEST ONES: *HOW TO RELEASE FEAR-BASED THINKING AND FEELING* AND *THE GOLDEN BOOK OF MELCHIZEDEK: HOW TO BECOME AN INTEGRATED CHRIST/BUDDHA IN THIS LIFETIME*! THEY ARE THE TWO BEST BOOKS I HAVE EVER WRITTEN. TRUST ME, GET THEM!

ALSO CHECK OUT THE 15 AUDIO ASCENSION ACTIVATION MEDITATION TAPES—ALL TAPED AT THE WESAK FESTIVALS. THEY ARE SO POWERFUL THEY WILL BLOW YOUR MIND! THEY WILL ACCELERATE YOUR ASCENSION PROCESS A THOUSANDFOLD, QUITE SERIOUSLY!

LASTLY COME TO THE NEXT WESAK CELEBRATION, YOU WILL ABSOLUTELY LOVE IT!

YES, THE FAMOUS "BURNING POTS," OR "NEW AGE CAMP-FIRE" AS I LIKE TO CALL THEM! JUST GET A SMALL COOKING POT. FILL IT WITH ABOUT AN INCH OF EPSOM SALT. THEN POUR RUBBING ALCOHOL INTO THE POT SO THE RUBBING

ALCOHOL IS ABOUT A HALF AN INCH ABOVE THE EPSOM SALT. PUT A HOT PLATE ON THE FLOOR IN THE ROOM YOU WANT TO CLEAN. PUT THE POT ON TOP OF THE PLATE SO AS NOT TO BURN THE RUG OR FLOOR AND JUST LIGHT A MATCH AND TOSS IT IN. IT WILL TAKE ABOUT TEN MINUTES TO BURN AND IS THE BEST WAY ON THE PLANET TO CLEAN THE PSYCHIC ATMOSPHERE OF ANY ROOM. I DO THEM ABOUT EVERY TWO WEEKS WITH SO MUCH GOING ON AT THE ACADEMY! BE SURE NOT TO PUT THE POT TOO CLOSE TO ANYTHING THAT CAN CATCH ON FIRE OF COURSE!

WARMEST REGARDS,
DR JOSHUA DAVID STONE

* *

41

"Did the Wesak Energy affect my Miscarriage?"

Dear Dr. Stone,

Thank you so much! Thank you for the love I felt shining through your message. I am honored, and let the tears that rolled down my cheeks as I read your love-filled message to me be my testament. I trust you, and Yes, I do want the books you mentioned.

I also want to ask you a unique personal question that I have been wanting to ask you for a while but have hesitated to bother you with it, but you of all people might have the best perspective since it concerns the Wesak energy. When I went to Wesak I was about nine weeks pregnant with my first child, one I have been waiting on, preparing for, for a long while. The timing seemed perfect for this child. I understood then why I had been waiting so long. My husband and I conceived in one of our most sacred places. So many things lined up. When I went to Wesak that too made sense for this baby. When I was there, I thought perhaps the baby had something to do with getting me there. He really wanted that experience as well. During the incredible meditations, I would focus energy to myself, my body, my process, as well as to my husband and to our land & home, shining the light on our mission and asking for guidance. I would focus energy toward my abdomen and the baby inside. When we were doing the Extraterrestrial meditation in particular (the biggest stretch for me), I realized how much energy the baby was absorbing on levels that I wasn't. I was absorbing/taking in so much incredible energy, I was surprised how much I could have and how much you could give. You don't hold back! You are an amazing, limitless gift! But at that moment during the ET meditation, when I realized the other levels the baby was getting that I wasn't, I felt a bit of separation and wondered if I would recognize/relate anymore to the entity being born unto me. It was an odd thought/sensation, not one I figured anyone else would understand. After I left Wesak I didn't think about this so much until three weeks later when my husband and I were at another very special place we love and go annually and I had a miscarriage there. I was so surprised! I didn't expect this at all. I was shocked and didn't understand. What changed? I didn't think this was the experience I was creating from the beginning. It seemed like something shifted in the process. It's been over a month now and I am a lot better emotionally and physically but still sad about the loss. I was so excited to finally be pregnant that it is a loss to be back at square one again. I know it isn't really square one but it is still a disappointment.

You may have nothing to say to me about this and that is completely o.k. It just perplexed me and I think the Wesak energy had something to do with it. Perhaps it makes sense to you.

Thank you again for EVERYTHING! I look forward to getting the books and thank you for the guidance. You are such a prolific writer that I didn't know which book to begin with.

I look forward to hearing from you again and reading your writings!

Blessings from me.

Dr. Stone's Reply:

Greetings, my Sweet Friend!

Thanks for your beautiful email and sharing! It is a pleasure having communication with someone like you with such heart and beautiful Christed Enthusiasm!

Thank you for trusting me in asking this question. Let me put this into the proper Christed perspective for you. What you must understand is that there are two ways of thinking in each person and only two. Each person thinks from his or her Spiritual/Christ/Buddha mind or each person thinks from his or her negative ego/fear-based/separative/lower-self mind! How you feel is caused by how you think, it is not caused by anything outside of self!

So, in terms of what occurred with the miscarriage, in total unconditional love and compassion, you must understand that there is faulty thinking going on a little bit and you intuitively knew this and that is why you have written. First off, meditations had nothing to do with the miscarriage. That was in the cards regardless of whether you went to Wesak or not!

Secondly, it is very important to see the higher wisdom of God and not second-guess God! There is always a reason and purpose for everything. You have heard the expression of course; this was a "blessing in disguise." The proper attitude to everything that happens in life is "Not my will but thine Oh Lord. Thank you for the lesson!" When perceived properly everything that occurs is a Spiritual Test, a Spiritual Lesson, an opportunity to grow, and a stepping stone for soul growth.

Thirdly, your baby did not die, for your true baby is not a physical body, it is a soul. That soul is still very much alive and may still choose to come as your child, however, the timing was not right as God saw it and this is why this occurred!

You have heard the expression; "God works in mysterious ways"! For example, one possible reason for what happened is that there is a Spiritual Maturation process you are now going through which God wants you to focus on first before having this child. You got very opened up at Wesak and God wants you now to study my books and get Right with self and Right with God first. He wants you to take this time for yourself now. Once your baby comes there will not be quite as much time to focus on building your proper Spiritual and Psychological foundation. The purpose of life is not to have a baby first; it is to realize God. Do you see the danger here? God wants you to have a little time to Spiritually mature. There is also a saying that God will always give this or something better! Thank God for this lesson! With total compassion in my heart, I say that sadness and disappointment, although understandable, are products of attachment. Did not Lord Buddha say in his Four Noble Truths that all suffering comes from attachment, all suffering comes from wrong points of view? You were attached, were you not? Make all things Preferences not Attachments. This way happiness becomes an inner state of mind, not dependent on having a baby or based on any outside thing. These are lessons you will learn through studying my books. Once you read my books, you are going to write me later and tell me why you see that this needed to happen. Now you see life with a very limited lens and not the full spectrum prism consciousness that God sees things with!

Your consciousness and hence your vision is also being colored by seeing through the negative ego and personality level mind and not your full Spiritual/Christ/Buddha consciousness! This is the reason for the sadness and disappointment. This is why I guided you to read my books even before you told me this! You are a very beautiful soul and God does not want you to get side tracked. He has given you the gift of a little time to work on your self Spiritually and Psychologically. You sensed that this was an evolved soul who wanted to come in. This soul wants you to catch up Spiritually!

There is also a saying that when the person is ready the teacher appears. Spirit and the Masters have sent you to me for Spiritual training; through my books, Wesak, Website, tapes and Academy services, so that you may find your full spiritual mission, puzzle piece, Spiritual Path, Ascension, and so on. This way the soul that comes into the future child you will have will be helped infinitely more Spiritually as well! Spiritual training is needed on your part! God has given you a gift and temporary delay only so you can do this

Study my books and all will be revealed! All that was happening was that the negative ego mind was questioning the wisdom of God! Who do you think has more wisdom, the illusionary negative ego that does not really even exist or God? This is a blessing from God and only a temporary delay for much higher Spiritual reasons than your personality level mind now understands. You, through this channeling, have been given a glimpse, understanding, and perspective on how God, Spirit, and the Masters would have you interpret this situation. Already you can feel the inner peace that comes when you learn to interpret life from God's mind and not the negative ego mind! You have been given your first Spiritual training in this regard. Study my books and God's infinite universe will open up to you and then you will be right with self and right with God and then you shall have your child. Does not the Bible say, "Seek ye the Kingdom of God and all things shall be added unto thee"?

So let it be written! So let it be done!

Much Love,
Your Eternal Spiritual Brother and Friend,
Dr Joshua David Stone

* *

42

"Is Christ the Governing Head of our Universe?"

Dear Dr. Stone,

Thank you for your earlier response, I'll not burden your time beyond this point. If you will, would you speak about Melchizedek's role in the universe? Am I clear in thinking Christ is the governing head of our universe? If so, what is Melchizedek's particular facet of authority?

Please forgive the intrusion Dr. Stone. Thank you again for your consideration. It's my thinking to start with *The Golden Book of Melchizedek*, is this advisable?

All the best,

Dr. Stone's Reply:

GREETINGS MY FRIEND!

CHRIST IS NOT THE HEAD OF THE UNIVERSE. CHRIST IS THE HEAD OF OUR PLANETARY HIERARCHY AND IS A REALIZED GALACTIC MASTER. MELCHIZEDEK IS A FULLY REALIZED UNIVERSAL MASTER ON THE WAY TO BECOMING A GOD REALIZED MASTER. SO, WE ARE DEALING WITH LEVELS HERE—PLANETARY, SOLAR, GALACTIC, UNIVERSAL, MULTI-UNIVERSAL, AND COSMIC OR GOD LEVEL! THIS IS WHY THERE ARE 352 LEVELS OF INITIATION TO REALIZE GOD! MY BOOKS WILL EXPLAIN ALL THIS.

THE GOLDEN BOOK OF MELCHIZEDEK THAT YOU MEN-TIONED, AND *THE COMPLETE ASCENSION MANUAL* WOULD BE THE BEST BOOKS TO START WITH FOR YOU. THEN *SOUL PSYCHOLOGY* AND *HOW TO RELEASE FEAR-BASED THINKING AND FEELING.* IT IS ESSENTIAL TO MASTER BOTH THE SPIRI-TUAL AND PSYCHOLOGICAL LEVELS OF SELF-REALIZATION AND THESE FOUR BOOKS WILL HELP YOU DO THIS. TRUST ME, MY FRIEND! YOU WILL LITERALLY NEVER BE THE SAME AFTER READING THESE BOOKS. THEY WILL LITERALLY REV-OLUTIONIZE YOUR CONSCIOUSNESS AND YOUR LIFE! THE BOOKS ARE ALL AVAILABLE FROM THE ACADEMY!

WARMEST REGARDS,
DR JOSHUA DAVID STONE

* *

43

"My Mother is Suffering from a Nervous Breakdown—Help!"

Dear Dr. Stone:

I am writing on behalf of my mother, whom is suffering from a severe nervous breakdown and panic attacks. We both have read your books and have visited Sai Baba, so we are spiritually open and aware. However, for the past two years my mother, since leaving my father, has become permanently anxious, panicky, isn't able to become calm and peaceful inside, and therefore works herself up to a greater degree.

Now, having decided that no miracle can save her, she has become in a critical state and is contemplating suicide. She insists that her state is not consciously self-induced and that she feels she has tried everything to become "normal" again. Her state results in her never leaving the house, unable to do anything except smoke cigarettes, and she can't read or watch TV for longer than half an hour.

I am nearly as desperate as she is for her to be able to function as she used to. Please, I would greatly appreciate it if you would be able to give advice or help in any way. Please get back to me as soon as possible.

Yours Sincerely,
With all my love,

Dr. Stone's Reply:

Greetings my friend!

Thanks for your email! Contrary to what your mother is saying, this is being created by her mind. Feelings and emotions come from the way one thinks. Even Sai Baba says, "Your mind creates bondage or your mind creates liberation." I have a book that I have written just for this purpose called *How to Release Fear-Based Thinking and Feeling*. It is only available from the Academy! This book, in conjunction with a tape called "The 18 point Cosmic Cleansing Meditation," would greatly help. I will also put her on our Interdimensional Prayer Altar to get the Masters working on her as well! She should also see a Psychologist or Counselor! She is just allowing the negative ego mind to run her ragged. Did not Sai Baba say, "God equals man minus ego"? There is nothing wrong with her except that she is thinking with her negative ego mind and not her Spiritual/Positive mind. This book and tape will help. Also, my book *Soul Psychology*! If necessary, have her see a psychiatrist and temporarily put her on medication or even a stay in a hospital if it is getting so serious where she is thinking about suicide! If she will follow my program this can be reprogrammed within 21 days, but she will have to study my two books that I have mentioned!

Pray constantly and ask the Masters to perform the Core Fear Matrix Removal Program all night while she sleeps and ask for this three times a day! They will pull all the fear programming, like weeds, out of her field, but she will have to study my books and listen to the tape or it won't hold. She needs to listen to the tape every day for 21 days. Ask her to make one final supreme effort to follow my program. I have brought thousands of people back from suicidal states to be totally normal and happy. She must be willing to fight and give it one more try using my books and tapes! Read her this letter! It is not only from me it is from God and the Masters. They want me to tell her that they will help as well. God wishes her to know that He has heard her prayers and answered them through this letter! If she really wants to recover and heal then she must not give up anymore, which is what she is doing, and must become a Spiritual Warrior and follow the program I have outlined!

The books are worth their weight in Gold! If she is serious about wanting to recover, this is way. God is now offering her a way home. The question is, does she have the eyes to see and the ears to hear to take advantage of the gift and way home God is now offering?

In the meantime, you can study the Website:

Warmest Regards,
Dr Joshua David Stone

* *

44

"Do the Stars and Planetary positions Affect Us?"

Dear Dr. Stone:

Do the stars and planetary positions really affect us in our body and soul? Do they also affect Buddhas?

Dr. Stone's Reply:

Greetings my friend!

You ask an interesting question! The stars definitely have an influence. Look at the effect the moon has on the oceans, tides, and on people's emotions! This is common knowledge to everyone. The thing you must understand is that the stars have an influence, however, we are not victims of the stars. For God created the Stars and we, in truth, are incarnations of God! There are some that let themselves be run by astrology in a type of victim consciousness, and this is not good! On the other side of the coin, others totally disregard astrology, saying it has no influence at all, which is not good either. Stars have more effect the more a person has victim consciousness. As one becomes a Master, or a Buddha as you say, astrology plays less and less a role, for a Master lets God guide them directly and creates their reality by their thoughts and prayers. I personally do not pay that much attention to astrology at this stage of my life, except for major aspects or the planning of major events. It is worth it for everyone to have an astrological horoscope done with a "qualified" reader, however, always remember that regardless of your sign your true purpose is to embody all of God, not just one sign. The influence of the Seven Great Rays of God has an even bigger influence than astrology!

Warmest Regards,
Dr Joshua David Stone

* *

45

About Melchizedek & Buddha

Dear Dr. Stone:

Brief me more about Lord Melchizedek and Lord Buddha.

Dr. Stone's Reply:

Greetings my friend!

Lord Melchizedek is the President of the entire universe that we live in! He is what is called in the inner plane Spiritual Government, *The Universal Logos*! He is in charge of the evolution of all beings on all planets in this universe. Of course, there are infinite numbers of universes in God's Creation. We live in just one! The theme of our universe is "Courage"! Each universe has a different theme!

Lord Buddha is the Spiritual President of our planet in the Spiritual Government on the inner plane. He is what is called, *The Planetary Logos*! He resides in Shambhalla! Each year in Mt. Shasta I hold a global festival honoring Lord Buddha and the coming together of East and West called the Wesak! Read about this on my Website, my friend!

Sincerely,
Dr Joshua David Stone

* *

46

On Manifestation

GREETINGS MY FRIEND!

I WILL PUT YOUR PRAYER REQUEST ON THE ACADEMY INTERDIMENSIONAL PRAYER ALTAR TO HELP AS WELL! THE LESSON HERE IS THAT PRAYER IS ALWAYS GOOD BUT "INTEGRATED PRAYER" IS BETTER. THIS MEANS PRAYER IS MOST EFFECTIVE WHEN ALL LEVELS ARE IN ALIGNMENT ON A SUPERCONSCIOUS, CONSCIOUS, SUBCONSCIOUS, AND PHYSICAL LEVEL! ALSO, WHEN THERE IS NO NEGATIVE EGO ASPECTS CONTAMINATING THE PRAYER—SUCH THINGS AS GUILT, DOUBTS, FEAR, WORRY, LACK OF FAITH, TRUST, PATIENCE, AND ON AND ON. I WOULD VERY HUMBLY RECOMMEND THAT YOU AND YOUR HUSBAND READ TWO BOOKS OF MINE, *HOW TO CLEAR THE NEGATIVE EGO* AND *THE GOLDEN BOOK OF MELCHIZEDEK*, WHICH ARE THE BEST TWO BOOKS OF THE ENTIRE SERIES OF 31 BOOKS I HAVE WRITTEN. THEY WILL COMPLETELY CLEAR YOU OF ALL THAT IS NOT OF GOD IN YOUR CONSCIOUSNESS! ALSO, I WOULD RECOMMEND ONE TAPE OF MINE CALLED "THE 18

POINT COSMIC CLEANSING MEDITATION," WHICH I WOULD RECOMMEND YOU LISTEN TO EVERY DAY OR EVERY OTHER DAY FOR 21 DAYS. ESPECIALLY READ THE CHAPTERS IN THE TWO BOOKS ON HOW THE NEGATIVE EGO SABOTAGES THE LAWS OF MANIFESTATION, AND THE 14 LEVELS OF MANIFESTATION IN *THE GOLDEN BOOK*. THE NEGATIVE EGO BOOK WILL HELP YOU CLEAR THE ENTIRE NEGATIVE EGO. FOR REMEMBER, YOUR THOUGHTS CREATE YOUR REALITY AS WELL. ONCE YOUR FIELDS ARE CLEARED OUT AND YOUR THOUGHTS AND EMOTIONS ARE 100% PURIFIED AND ARE TOTALLY CHRISTED, MANIFESTATION WILL OCCUR MUCH MORE QUICKLY! SPIRIT AND THE MASTERS WISH YOU TO STUDY THIS WORK AND TO REALIZE THAT THIS IS A BLESSING IN DISGUISE, FOR THIS SPIRITUAL TEST HAS LED YOU TO ASK FOR THE HELP YOU NEED. THE ANSWER THAT YOU HAVE BEEN GIVEN IS THE ANSWER YOU SEEK, WHICH WILL SOLVE THIS LESSON AND BRING YOU INFINITELY MORE IF YOU HAVE THE EYES TO SEE AND THE EARS TO HEAR OF THE PROFUNDITY OF THE GIFT YOU HAVE BEEN GIVEN IN TERMS OF THE GUIDANCE SHARED. THESE BOOKS WILL BRING YOU A PEACE THAT PASSETH UNDERSTANDING AND, IN A VERY SIMPLE AND EASY TO UNDERSTAND WAY, HELP YOU TO NOT ONLY MASTER THIS SPIRITUAL TEST BUT ALL OTHERS IN THE FUTURE.

THESE TWO BOOKS ARE ONLY AVAILABLE FROM THE ACADEMY AND ARE VERY EASY TO READ. LITERALLY EVERY PERSON WHO HAS READ THEM TELLS ME THEY ARE THE BEST BOOKS THEY HAVE EVER READ, WHICH IS NO SMALL STATEMENT!

WARMEST REGARDS,
DR JOSHUA DAVID STONE

* *

47

"My Relationship Didn't Work Out. Do I Forget About It?"

Dear Dr. Stone:

My relationship has not worked out for me. Should I forget about it?

Please reply.

Dr. Stone's Reply:

Greetings my Friend!

You should definitely not forget about it. God is trying to teach you some lessons. Forgetting about it does not learn the lesson. The reason they are not working out is your need to learn to become more right with self and right with God first! Then your relationships will work out better! Study my book *Soul Psychology*. Study my Website and read all the free articles! I even have a book on Ascension and Romantic Relationships!

The cause of all problems is the negative ego mind. Learn to master your thoughts, emotions, and negative ego in service of God and unconditional love! Become more Self Realized. There is a Spiritual adage that says, "One should never leave a relationship until you have learned the lessons of the relationship, otherwise you are likely to repeat them again"! Learn from these relationships and work on self to become Self Realized. The greatest Spiritual Masters are able to be in relationships and retain their self-mastery! Relationships are the greatest test for Spiritual Growth! They can be difficult, but who said God Realization and becoming a Spiritual Master in all areas of life is easy! More Spiritual study is needed, that is all!

Warmest Regards,
Dr Joshua David Stone

* *

48

"How Do I Get this Message Across?"

Dear Dr. Stone:

What is the best way of dealing with a person with whom you are trying to give a message like "talent and time should be used not wasted"?

Dr. Stone's Reply:

Greetings my Friend!

The best way to give such a message is with unconditional love and nonattachment. Also, be sure it is even appropriate to give the feedback, for if the person is not open to hearing it sometimes certain things are better off left unsaid. Sometimes a prayer to God and the Masters would be even better. Or say the prayer first, which might help the person to be more open to hearing the feedback. Also, always share things by saying something nice first, otherwise they are likely to be defensive or ego sensitive! Timing is also important. Wait for a time when things are positive. Say it in a diplomatic and tactful way, not in a critical way. Say it in a way that builds them up, not knocks them down!

Warmest Regards,
Dr Joshua David Stone

* *

49

Question on Initiations
and Integration

Hello Dr. Stone,

I recently purchased all your books and will be holding ascension classes in my home. The reason I'm writing is I need your help and clarification.

I was just told that I am a "6th level initiate holding a steady 85% light quotient." However, I intuitively do not feel this. I feel that I have just taken my 3rd level initiation. However, when I talk to my husband, he feels that the other information is true too. Is it possible to be a 6th level initiate holding 85% light and still be taking/working on my 3rd level? All my life people have told me that I have a very high vibration, that I hold a lot of light. Psychics have told me many times that I didn't have to come here in this lifetime, all of which would validate the 6th level and does resonate with me, but again, I intuitively feel 3rd level and my tarot cards have indicated this as well. How can this be? Is this a test?

I truly need to be clear on this in order to start/lead an ascension class. If I'm not even clear…

Also, I do the Ascension Meditation and Treatment every day and now I find confusion in what I am asking and intending for.

So, Dr. Stone, will you please help me to understand?

Thank you so much!

Blessings to you and Wistancia.

Dr. Stone's Reply:

GREETINGS MY FRIEND!

THANKS FOR YOUR EMAIL! I AM SO PLEASED YOU ARE ENJOYING MY BOOKS, MY FRIEND! LET ME SEE IF I CAN EXPLAIN THIS FOR YOU! IT IS A TOTALLY UNDERSTANDABLE QUESTION AND PROCESS AND IT IS GOOD YOU HAVE WRITTEN ME ABOUT THIS!

WHAT IS GOING ON IS THAT YOUR SPIRITUAL BODY IS AT THE SIXTH LEVEL, HOWEVER, IN TERMS OF YOUR INTEGRATION OF ALL THESE INITIATIONS, YOU ARE STILL PROCESSING THEM IN YOUR MENTAL, EMOTIONAL AND PHYSICAL BODIES. THIS IS TRUE OF EVERYONE, HOWEVER, YOU ARE INTUITIVE AND INSIGHTFUL TO REALIZE THIS, WHERE MOST ARE NOT. WHEN THE LORD BUDDHA BRINGS FORTH HIS ROD OF INITIATION IT IS DONE IN CONSIDERATION OF THE SPIRITUAL BODY ONLY, WHICH MAKES INITIATION MORE OF A PRODUCT OF LIGHT QUOTIENT AND NOTHING

ELSE. HARD TO BELIEVE BUT TRUE! SO, A PERSON CAN BE A SEVENTH DEGREE INITIATE, STILL GREATLY RUN BY THE NEGATIVE EGO, AND STILL IS AN EMOTIONAL VICTIM. I KNOW PEOPLE WHO ARE BEYOND THE 12TH INITIATION WHO ARE EMOTIONAL VICTIMS, WITH NO JUDGMENT INTENDED. THIS DOES NOT APPLY TO YOU, BUT, WITH NO JUDGMENT INTENDED, SOME OF THE MOST DISTURBED AND CORRUPTED PEOPLE I KNOW HAVE TAKEN VERY HIGH LEVELS OF INITIATIONS. TRY AND FIGURE THAT OUT.

THIS ALL DOES NOT APPLY TO YOU, HOWEVER, I AM JUST TRYING TO MAKE A POINT THAT IT IS ONE THING TO TAKE AN INITIATION BUT ANOTHER THING TO INTEGRATE IT INTO YOUR MENTAL AND EMOTIONAL VEHICLE. DO YOU SEE WHY I HAVE WRITTEN SO MANY BOOKS ON SPIRITUAL PSYCHOLOGY?

THIS IS WHY YOU SHOULD READ MY BOOKS *HOW TO RELEASE FEAR-BASED THINKING AND FEELING* AND *THE GOLDEN BOOK OF MELCHIZEDEK: HOW TO BECOME AN INTEGRATED CHRIST/BUDDHA IN THIS LIFETIME!* ALSO, READ *INTEGRATED ASCENSION, HOW TO CLEAR THE NEGA- TIVE EGO*, AND, OF COURSE, *SOUL PSYCHOLOGY!* THE MAS- TERS ASKED ME TO WRITE THESE BOOKS TO HELP INITIATES INTEGRATE THEIR ASCENSION INTO THEIR FOUR LOWER BODIES.

SO, BOTH ARE TRUE. YOU HAVE TAKEN THE SIXTH BUT ARE STILL WORKING ON INTEGRATION OF THOSE INITIATIONS. MOST LIGHTWORKERS THINK THAT IF THEY TAKE AN INITI- ATION THAT MEANS THAT HAVE AUTOMATICALLY ACHIEVED IT ON ALL LEVELS, AND THIS IS 100% NOT TRUE.

JUST THE OPPOSITE. THIS IS WHY THE SPIRITUAL MOVE-
MENT IS SO FILLED WITH NEGATIVE EGO, GLAMOUR AND A
GREAT DEAL OF CORRUPTION AND PERSONAL AGENDAS, TO
BE QUITE HONEST! THIS IS WHY THE MASTERS, IN TRUTH,
ARE NOT INTERESTED IN ASCENSION! THEY ARE INTER-
ESTED IN "INTEGRATED" ASCENSION! NOW DO YOU SEE?

WARMEST REGARDS,
DR JOSHUA DAVID STONE

* *

50

On the Issue of Worshipping Money

Well dear one, I've beamed down!

Trust, affirmation, faith, etc. in God and the Masters did little to assist a smooth run! The anaesthetic was the worst ever and it is taking me some while to recover. I wonder also why I wasn't able to receive a visit from a friend in spirit (even a master or two!) whilst "under." I was in deep space and connected at some high level having conversation with a direct link at some distance. Most peculiar. Would you know what that was?

Also, I am having trouble with the manifestation theory. While reading your wonderful Melchizedek book, I came across this "law" but also read about your disapproval of students who apparently "worship" money and activate the laws of prosperity. How can these two be in conflict? Are we or are we not meant to manifest what we need? If so, why do you consider it "worshiping" money?

Much love,

Dr. Stone's Reply:

Greetings!

Glad you recovered!

As to the money issue, you misunderstand. There is nothing wrong with making money or manifesting what you need. Just put God before money! Don't make money your God! I am totally into being a millionaire, and pray for help making money and increasing business all the time. I am just not attached to it. It is a preference not an attachment! God must come before everything, even people and children! Ponder on this! Abraham had to almost kill his son Isaac because he put Isaac before God. He was only spared from having to do this when he put God first! For example, would you steal for money, or break your integrity or code of ethics to have money? If the answer is, "Of course not," then you are putting God first! Would you get angry over money and create separation over money in relationships? If the answer is "No," then you have your head screwed on straight! That is all. Many lightworkers say they put God first but they don't. For example, they would never help someone if they didn't get paid! I think you get the point!

Much Love,
Dr Joshua David Stone

* *

51

"I Discovered Ramayana and Mahabharta are 'mere' Epics—Is this True?"

Dear Dr. Stone:

Sir, I am a young person working as an engineer. Recently I discovered that Ramayana and Mahabharta are mere epics, sheer imagination of people. It has come to me as a great shock and I am in total confusion. If such a lie could exist on earth for such a long period then what is true? We are taught to follow truth, kindness, etc. in life, but just see the politicians and it seems the way to life is only that which gives you success, nothing just or unjust. There doesn't seem to be any proof of life after death and further, their relation to so-called karmas. In such a state, finding the right way is completely confusing.

Please help me know what is right and why. Will you, please?

Dr. Stone's Reply:

Greetings my friend!

Thanks for your email. I must explain to you, my good friend, that although some of these two books are fiction and not fact, there are some aspects that are true and you must realize this. Krishna and Rama were, for an absolute fact, Spiritual Masters who lived on the earth! So to say these books are total imagination and fiction is not true. It is true their lives were embellished upon, and it is good you have this spiritual discernment, however, it is important to not "throw the baby out with the bath water" as the saying goes!

In terms of recognizing the existence of God and the truth that death does not exist, it is the most obvious thing in the world if you will be still, quiet your mind, and transcend all negative ego thoughts. Sai Baba has said "God equals man minus ego"! It is because your mind, with no judgment intended, is filled with so may negative ego thoughts instead of God thoughts that you cannot perceive and interpret life correctly. The negative ego, or lower-self mind, is like a dark set of glasses that makes us think that all that exists is what we can experience with our five senses. This is literally only 1/10th of all that exists in the true nature of things!

My friend, study my books and Website and read all the free articles and information. The obviousness of the existence of God and Spiritual things will be as tangible as the things in your home. It is no accident that you have written me, for your soul is seeking the truth and your Higher Self, God, and the Masters have led you to me in this moment to find the answers you seek. I am asking no money of you, my friend, yet I am offering you everything! Just study my Website and read the articles I have written and the truth of my humble words, which have been inspired by God and the inner plane Masters, will be unmistakable to you. I would recommend that you read my book *Soul Psychology*. This will help you get more right with self and right with God in your own consciousness, which will help you to see with clear eyes. Do not underestimate the importance and significance of this moment! God has heard the unspoken prayer of your heart and soul and has guided you to me. There is a saying in Metaphysics; "Once the student is ready the teacher appears"!

Study my Website and it will lead you to find inner peace and how to live a Spiritual Life, be successful, be of service, and how to fulfill the mission and purpose you came to fulfill! Do not let the negative ego mind sabotage you by not listening to the guidance I give you. For what I offer you is totally free and all I want for you is God Realization and happiness. You are in need of Spiritual training, that is all. God and the Masters are offering this to you now. This is not imagination I gave you now but tangible fact! In total humbleness and humility, you are now speaking to a living Spiritual Master on earth! This is not the thing of imagination but a thing of truth! Take a chance now that the things I say just might be true, and study my Website and start training yourself with my free teachings and you will then receive the Spiritual training you need to find the truth you seek. Your discernment about these books is excellent. Now be open to studying books that are 100% true. I offer these to you now, my friend!

Warmest Regards,
Dr Joshua David Stone

* *

52

Paranormal Experiences

Dear Dr. Stone:

When I once went to visit an ailing relative, I saw my own subtle form come out of my physical body, comfort my relative, and come back into me. I have also had many other paranormal experiences. For the past year, I have been taking psychiatric treatment for schizophrenia (hearing voices, delusions, etc). This happened before I started treatment. Can you enlighten me as to what really happened? Was my mind playing games on me? I have been doing Japa for the past three years and am a spiritually inclined person.

Dr. Stone's Reply:

Greetings my Friend!

Thanks for your question. Yes, your experience of one of your subtle bodies comforting a relative did take place and does happen all the time. Most people just are not aware it is happening. When we sleep at night, for example, our different bodies—Spiritual, mental, emotional, etheric—all travel to different planes of existence. We are all, in truth, multi-dimensional in nature. If you think about it, the Infinite Creation of God is nothing more than God splitting Himself into infinite numbers of pieces and incarnating into material existence, which is, in truth, you, and I and every single person in this world and all others. It is a grand experiment of all these aspects of God with free choice now in the process of returning home! We, as incarnations of God and microcosmic copies of God, have the ability to split our consciousness and bodies into infinite numbers of pieces as well. The more evolved we become Spiritually, the greater the number. This also happens unconsciously as well, which you were a witness to. Medical doctors will tell you that the voices you are hearing is schizophrenia, when, in truth, they are just inner plane Spiritual beings. Traditional medicine will tell you this is not real, however, with no judgment intended, it is they who are living in the hallucination and delusion and not you, my friend. Your lesson is to learn to attune to the Spiritual plane and not the Astral plane. The Astral plane is where all the lower-self, unconscious, and darker or negative beings live. This is nothing you want to listen to. You must learn to master your thoughts, feelings, and emotions, and get rid of all negative ego, lower-self thoughts and emotions. You must learn to only think and have Spiritual feelings, emotions and behaviors, and keep your attention only on the positive, the light, the love, and on God. Then you can attune at all times to the Spiritual Plane and communicate directly with the inner plane Ascended Masters as I do! It is good you chant the Name of God, for this a good practice!

Study my Website and all the free articles and mediations and services there. Study my book *Soul Psychology*, for it is not necessary to hold on to this label of "schizophrenia." You are perfectly fine, my friend, you need to have Spiritual training to master your energies, that is all. This is a process, my friend. It is good you are under a doctor's care, however, move toward the idea and goal of becoming a Spiritual Master and then you will not need this label or have any negative symptoms. You are suffering from lack of Spiritual Training, that is all. That is the only label God and the Ascended Masters gives you!

Warmest Regards,
Dr Joshua David Stone

* *

53

On Types of Spiritual Vision

Dear Dr. Stone:

Greetings!

What is the difference between a "spiritual eye" experience and a vision within or without the mind?

Much Love,

Dr. Stone's Reply:

GREETINGS!

YOU ASK AN INTERESTESTING QUESTION THAT VERY FEW PEOPLE UNDERSTAND. THERE ARE DIFFERENT KINDS OF SPIRITUAL VISION AND ASPECTS TO THE THIRD EYE. THERE IS SPIRITUAL UNDERSTANDING, WHICH IS ONE FACET. THERE IS PSYCHOLOGICAL UNDERSTANDING, WHICH IS ANOTHER. THERE IS THE ABILITY TO IMAGINE OR VISUALIZE

OR RECEIVE IMAGES, WHICH IS ANOTHER. THERE IS CLAIR-VOYANCE, WHICH IS ANOTHER. MANY PEOPLE, FOR EXAMPLE, COULD BE CLAIRVOYANT BUT HAVE ALMOST NO SPIRITUAL EYE OPENING OR ANY UNDERSTANDING ON THE PSYCHOLOGICAL LEVEL. THIS IS WHY I HAVE COINED THE TERM MYSTIC AND OCCULT VISION.

SO A VISION WITHIN THE MIND IS PART OF THE SPIRITUAL EYE. ANOTHER ASPECT MIGHT BE ONE WHO IS A VISION-ARY. I AM AMAZED HOW MANY PEOPLE HAVE MYSTIC VISION, WHICH MOST PEOPLE THINK IS WHAT THE THIRD EYE IS, AND ARE BLIND IN TERMS OF OCCULT VISION AND PSYCHOLOGICAL VISION. THIS TENDS TO CORRUPT THEIR MYSTIC VISION. MY THIRD EYE IS VERY LARGE BECAUSE MY OCCULT AND PSYCHOLOGICAL VISION IS SO DEVELOPED.

I HOPE THIS EXPLAINS THIS. I THINK IT IS A GOOD UNDER-STANDING AND ONE THAT VERY FEW UNDERSTAND!

MUCH LOVE,
DR JOSHUA DAVID STONE

✳ ✳

54

"What is 'I Am Fixed Design'?"

Hi Joshua,

A quick question. I like the mantra you have in one of your books:

I am the soul
I am the light divine
I am love
I am will
I am fixed design

I don't understand the last line. Can you explain it to me?

Thanks in advance.

Dr. Stone's Reply:

Greetings my friend!

Thanks for your email. This is a good question! It means "Everything is in Divine Order as God created it"! See!

Warmest Regards,
Dr Joshua David Stone

* *

55

"Is Ascension for Adolescents?"

Dear Dr. Joshua David Stone,

I was wondering if Ascension is only for adults or is it for adolescents as well.

P.S. Have you ascended, and if so, how does one ascend in this lifetime?

Dr. Stone's Reply:

GREETINGS MY FRIEND!

YES, ASCENSION IS FOR EVERYONE OF ALL AGES, FOR THAT IS THE PURPOSE YOU HAVE INCARNATED INTO THIS WORLD FOR—TO BECOME GOD-REALIZED, ASCEND, AND BE OF SERVICE! I HAVE FULLY ASCENDED, YES.

TO LEARN HOW TO ASCEND, READ MY BOOKS *SOUL PSY-CHOLOGY, THE COMPLETE ASCENSION MANUAL, HOW TO RELEASE FEAR-BASED THINKING AND FEELING,* AND *THE*

GOLDEN BOOK OF MELCHIZEDEK: HOW TO BECOME AN INTEGRATED CHRIST/BUDDHA IN THIS LIFETIME! THESE BOOKS ARE ALL AVAILABLE FROM THE ACADEMY.

ALSO, WORK WITH MY 15 AUDIO ASCENSION ACTIVATION MEDITATION TAPES, ALSO AVAILABLE FROM THE ACADEMY. THE BOOKS ALONG WITH THESE TAPES, AND POSSIBLY IN THE FUTURE COMING TO ONE OF MY WESAK CELEBRA-TIONS IN MT. SHASTA, WILL HELP YOU TO ACHIEVE THIS GOAL. DO NOT UNDERESTIMATE THE SIGNIFICANCE OF THIS MOMENT. YOU HAVE FOUND, BY THE GRACE OF GOD AND THE MASTERS, I VERY HUMBLY TELL YOU, THE MOST ADVANCED SPIRITUAL AND PSYCHOLOGICAL TEACHINGS ON THIS PLANET THAT ARE VERY EASY TO UNDERSTAND AND PRACTICAL. TAKE ADVANTAGE OF IT, MY FRIEND!

WARMEST REGARDS,
DR JOSHUA DAVID STONE

* *

56

"How Can I Go Deep Within Myself?"

Dear Dr. Stone:

Please show me a way so that I can go deep within myself.

Dr. Stone's Reply:

Greetings my friend!

Thank you for your question! I will give you two 20-minute meditations to do. One will be a preliminary and one a deeper more Spiritual one!

Make a vocal payer to God, Christ, the Holy Spirit, Lord Buddha, Lord Krishna, Sai Baba, and the Ascended Master Djwhal Khul to anchor within you the "Core Fear Matrix Removal Program" and to remove all core fear and negative ego thinking within you! Then sit very quietly for 20 minutes and feel a latticework of light being anchored within you! Then feel the Masters pulling out of your crown chakra all your negative ego and fear-based programming, like pulling weeds out of a beautiful garden! Has not Sai Baba said "God equals man minus ego"?

Secondly, when this meditation is done, call forth God, Christ, the Holy Spirit, Lord Buddha, and Lord Krishna! Ask to be taken to Lord Buddha's ashram on the inner plane and to sit in his Ascension Seat in Shambhalla! You will immediately feel your Spiritual body travel there and you will feel a stream of Spiritual current plow down though and around you like a gigantic pillar of light and Ascension Column! Sit and bathe in this energy! You may either be silent or if you prefer you can also chant the names of God or name of God— you choose. When done, sit in the silence and enjoy the Spiritual ecstasy, bliss, joy, and love of God!

Peace be with you, my God-seeking friend! Study my Website for meditations and articles.

Warmest Regards,
Dr Joshua David Stone

✳ ✳

57

On Reincarnation

Dear Dr. Stone:

Hello, I had a brief question on your view on reincarnation.

I was born normal, then had an accident, then brain damage. The brain does not register much, although once smart. Like the person disappeared and now there is something else there, just a blankness not a human. I didn't think this could happen. I thought you were guaranteed your natural intelligence for life. I was walking across the street and got hit by a cyclist, and then my faculties went blank. So I just wonder about rebirth and how can I be born human again next life with the basic human faculties that everyone else has. Do we get a new human "package" each life with a normal human head and brain that works right? I don't know why my faculties had to go to nothing.

So I was just wondering, what are the causes for a normal basic human rebirth with normal human intelligence? Also, if I die with dementia, what is left to carry over? I know these are odd questions. I wanted to get the Buddhist perspective. Any feedback is helpful.

Sincerely,

Dr. Stone's Reply:

GREETINGS MY FRIEND!

THANKS FOR YOUR EMAIL. I AM NOT BUDDHIST BUT I WOULD BE HONORED TO ANSWER YOUR QUESTION. I AM A UNIVERSALIST! I BELIEVE IN ALL RELIGIONS, ALL SPIRITUAL PATHS, ALL MYSTERY SCHOOLS, AND ALL PATHS BACK TO GOD! ONE MIGHT SAY I AM A MASTER OF SYNTHESIS!

THE ACCIDENT YOU SUFFERED IS JUST A LESSON, NOTHING MORE, AND NOTHING LESS. WHEN YOU PASS ON TO THE SPIRITUAL WORLD ALL YOUR FACULTIES WILL BE TOTALLY PERFECT AND NORMAL. YOUR SOUL AND ALL YOUR SPIRITUAL AND PSYCHOLOGICAL FACULTIES ARE, IN TRUTH, STILL PERFECT, BUT BEING INCARNATED INTO A PHYSICAL VEHICLE THAT HAS BEEN DAMAGED, YOU ARE EXPERIENCING THE REALITY OF THE BODY ON A THIRD-DIMENSIONAL LEVEL. JUST TEMPORARY, MY FRIEND. SO HAVE PEACE OF MIND. IT IS A SPIRITUAL TEST, AS YOU SAY!

IN TERMS OF YOUR NEXT LIFE, IF YOU NEED ONE, YOU WILL HAVE A PERFECTLY HEALTHY PHYSICAL BODY. YOU HAVE NO KARMA TO CAUSE YOU TO HAVE TO DO THIS AGAIN! TRY TO MAKE AS MUCH SPIRITUAL GROWTH AS YOU CAN THIS LIFETIME. LOOK AT CHRISTOPHER REEVES AND THE WONDERFUL EXAMPLE HE IS SETTING FOR THE WORLD! FOCUS ON

WHAT YOU *CAN* DO, NOT ON WHAT YOU *CAN'T* DO. REMAIN POSITIVE IN YOUR ATTITUDE. READ MY BOOK *SOUL PSY-CHOLOGY!* IT WILL BRING YOU GREAT PEACE OF MIND! YOUR ATTITUDE AND THOUGHTS CREATE YOUR REALITY AND HOW YOU FEEL, NOT THE HEALTH OR DISEASE OF YOUR PHYSICAL BODY OR ANYTHING OUTSIDE OF SELF!

SPIRIT IS GUIDING YOU TO ME TO STUDY MY TEACHINGS, FOR GOD HAS HEARD YOUR PRAYERS AND THIS IS THE PATH THAT CAN HELP YOU GRADUATE EVEN FURTHER THIS LIFE-TIME WITH THE LIMITATIONS AND CROSSES THAT YOU BEAR. DO NOT UNDERESTIMATE THE IMPORTANCE OF THIS MOMENT. STUDY ALL THE FREE ARTICLES AND MEDITA-TIONS ON MY WEBSITE!

WARMEST REGARDS,
DR JOSHUA DAVID STONE

* *

58

Dr. Stone Answers Various Questions

GREETINGS MY FRIEND!

THANKS FOR YOUR LETTER AND KIND WORDS. IT IS UNRE-
ALISTIC TO THINK ANYONE YOU WRITE WOULD HAVE TIME
TO ANSWER SO MANY QUESTIONS. I WILL ANSWER A FEW OF
THE MORE IMPORTANT ONES, MY FRIEND, AS TIME PERMITS!

NO SOUL EXTENSION EVER DIES, SO YOU NEVER NEED TO
BE CONCERNED ABOUT THIS. DJWHAL WAS TALKING
ABOUT THE PERSONALITY OF THE PHYSICAL FORM IN
THAT STATEMENT. THE SOUL EXTENSION INHABITING THE
FORM NEVER EVER DIES, SO BE NOT CONCERNED!

DIVINE DISPENSATIONS DO AS THEY SAY DIFFERENTLY FOR
EACH PERSON, AS KARMIC LAW PERMITS FOR THAT PERSON.

ALL UNIVERSES AT SOME POINT STARTED PHYSICAL, BUT
SOME HAVE EVOLVED BEYOND THAT. COULD BE A TRILLION

YEARS OF BRAHMA AGO. ALL GO THROUGH THE SAME PROCESS.

THERE IS A SOURCE FOR EACH COSMIC DAY, HOWEVER, THERE ARE INFINITE COSMIC DAYS, SO AN INFINITE NUMBER OF SOURCES! ALL TOGETHER THEY UNIFY IN GOD!

GUIDES DIRECT US TO CLASSES, BUT SO DOES OUR OWN SOUL, OUR HIGHER SELF AND MONAD, AND THE CHOHAN OF EACH RAY!

WHAT WAS SAID ABOUT YOUR EVOLUTION BEING LIMITED BY 1000 SOULS WHO CAME WITH YOU IS UNTRUE. NO OTHER PERSON STOPS YOUR EVOLUTION!

IN TERMS OF LOVED ONES, THERE IS NO SUCH THING AS DEATH AND AS LONG AS THERE IS LOVE AND MUTUAL CONSENT YOU WILL SEE LOVED ONES WHEN YOU DIE AND CAN VISIT LOVED ONES AT ALL LEVELS AND STAGES. REMEMBER, ON THE INNER PLACE YOU TRAVEL WITH THOUGHT INSTANTLY AND THERE IS NO TIME OR SPACE. SO LOVED ONES CAN BE CONTACTED AS QUICKLY AS THE BLINK OF AN EYE IF THEY ARE AVAILABLE AND WANT TO PICK UP THE PHONE SO TO SPEAK!

WARMEST REGARDS,
DR JOSHUA DAVID STONE

* *

59

On Clearing Negative Thoughts

Dear Dr. Stone:

I can't concentrate with my prayers. And also, I am doubting with my family members. Always thinking negative thoughts.

Dr. Stone's Reply:

Greetings my friend!

As Sai Baba says, "Your mind creates bondage or your mind creates liberation"! Your thoughts create reality. One of the single most important lessons of life is mastering your thoughts. By learning to do this you can create only positive Spiritual feelings and emotions and behavior. It is all caused by thought! What you must understand is that every person has two minds. A negative ego mind and a spiritual mind. A lower-self mind and higher-self mind. God equals man minus ego! To realize God you must get rid of all the negative ego thoughts. Just push them out of your consciousness and replace them with positive ones. Do positive affirmations and visualizations.

Chant the Holy Names of God. An idle mind is the devil's workshop! If you practice what I say, within 21 days you can make a habit of being positive! You need to read my book *Soul Psychology*! There are also wonderful affirmations in there you need to work with. Study all the free articles on my Website!

Trust in my guidance and you will be able to quickly master this lesson and achieve inner peace! You are letting the negative ego/fear-based/separative mind run your life. You must be the captain of your ship, take command, and stop this mutiny! God has placed you on earth to learn these lessons. God is speaking to you now through me, reminding you of this in a loving way and guiding you how to master this. God guided you to write this letter to me so He could speak to you! Trust in these words for they will bring you a peace that passeth understanding!

Warmest Regards,
Dr Joshua David Stone

* *

60

"My Teenage Daughter is really Depressed, How Can I Help Her?"

Greetings my Friend!

Thanks for your email! Yes, it is good you have written. I have a number of ideas. It is good you are studying my book *Soul Psychology*, for in mastering this information within yourself you will be able to use it to help your daughter. What is unusual about my work is that it is not only the most cutting-edge work you will find in the field of Spiritual Psychology and Ascension, it is also very easy to understand and is very practical. Even your daughter can understand and use it. You should have her work with the affirmations in that book and with a lot of the exercises and techniques.

Depression stems from giving up, and that is what she has done on a subconscious level. She must learn to claim her personal power and self-mastery, and master her thoughts, emotions, and negative ego mind. You must also obtain my book called *How to Release Fear-Based Thinking and Feeling: An In-depth Study of Spiritual Psychology*! It is essential you read this book. These two books will give you the information you need to master this lesson.

Secondly, I would recommend you have a channeling session with my wife Wistancia and speak to the Masters about your daughter. Also, get a clearing session for your daughter to remove all implants, elementals, and imbalanced energies. This will greatly help as well!

I have a tape called "The 18 Point Mt. Shasta Cosmic Cleansing Meditation" which would greatly help as well. You both could listen to it together!

I would also bring your daughter to the "Iridescent Diamond Heart Wesak"! It will create a transformation within her that will passeth understanding! She needs to get firmly on her Spiritual Path; I am guided to share with you that this would greatly help!

Warmest Regards,
Dr Joshua David Stone

* *

61

On the Teachings of Dr. Stone
and Sai Baba

Greetings my friend!

Thanks for your email. I am so pleased you have found the Website! It is indeed Spirit and the Masters who have guided you there. Thank you for your straightforward question and I will give you a straightforward answer. My main work is with the Ascended Masters. I am a point man for the Ascended Masters on Earth. Read on the Website the section called "My Spiritual Mission" and you will see my purpose is to be a point man for the Ascended Masters, one of the 12 Prophets of Melchizedek on Earth, and to embody the Holy Spirit's energy on Earth! I have also been given future Spiritual leadership of the Second Ray inner plane Synthesis Ashram of Djwhal Khul, which I will share with Lord Maitreya and Master Kuthumi.

You must understand, however, my Spiritual Mission is in part one of Synthesis! This is why I have written a 40 volume Easy to Read Encyclopedia! This is why I have written about all the Masters, all the

Angels, all the Elohim, and all the Christed Extraterrestrials. This being the case, I would remiss to not write about Sai Baba as well!

In terms of Sai Baba, I have read all the reports. This is a lesson in Spiritual Discernment for Lightworkers! I am not saying some of what is written may not be true, however, the reports of this Master being totally corrupt are 100% not true. Jesus was crucified 2000 years and 2000 years later Sai Baba is being crucified over the Internet. Not everything you are reading is true and accurate. Be very discerning! As the Master Jesus said, "Judge not that ye not be judged" and "He that hath no sin cast the first stone"! It is also important to not "throw the baby out with the bathwater." There are some dark forces at work here that you are also not aware of that are coming from the other side as well. So, my guidance is to just be aware of both sides. Not all that is being said over the Internet is accurate.

So, my work is with the Ascended Masters and the truth from all Religions, all Masters, all Mystery Schools, and all Spiritual Teachers!

You will find great truth in the Academy Website and in all my books. You are really in for a treat!

Warmest Regards,
Dr Joshua David Stone

* *

62

"Will I Meet my Late Husband again?"

Dear Dr. Stone:

Whenever I need help I call on my late husband and he finds a solution to my problems. I feel that we are soul mates. I feel his presence in the house and find comfort. Will I one day meet him in the next birth?

Dr. Stone's Reply:

Greetings my Friend!

It is good that you have remained connected with your husband even though he has passed on to the Spirit world. You understand that there is no such thing as death and this is good! In terms of meeting him in your next birth—that will depend on your karma, his karma, each of your soul choices, and God's will! Your goal should be to achieve liberation so then you would have more choices that are available to you. You will see him on the inner plane if he is not incarnated! Eventually you will meet as long as love exists and it is both of your soul choice to do so. That I can say for sure!

Warmest Regards
Dr Joshua David Stone

* *

63

Dr. Stone answers some Questions

Question: *What do you consider is the most vital and important issue at this moment?*

Answer: The most vital and important issue on this planet is learning to transcend the negative ego mind and learning to be integrated and balanced on the Spiritual Path! Very few people understand that there are two ways of thinking in the world and only two. Lightworkers think they understand the negative ego but they do not! One cannot realize God without transcending the negative ego mind, no matter what level of Initiation a person is at! This is why all that are reading this should read my books *Soul Psychology* and *How to Release Fear-Based Thinking and Feeling: An In-depth Study of Spiritual Psychology*! The second one is only available from the Academy!

Q: *What would you like to say about the critical mass and its effect on the planet?*

A: Many are awakening, more in their Spiritual bodies than in their psychological selves, which gets back to this issue of lack of integration and knowing how to ground Spirituality on a mental, emotional, etheric, physical and earthly level. The Critical Mass is working like the Hundredth Monkey Syndrome. It is beginning to spread around the world. Spiritual ignition is taking place, but not integrated Spirituality yet! The world is still lagging behind in this area! The Masters have actually slowed things down a bit because of this!

Q: *Politics, the world economy, and environmental issues show that the world is very fragile. Can there be a breakthrough or will there be a breakdown?*

A: This is a difficult question to answer for it is multifaceted. In some areas, we will have some breakthroughs, however, in other areas we are having a total break down. Greedy oil companies, electric companies and so on will not let true New Age technology in because present forms of energy would become outdated. In the future, Christed Extraterrestrials will be landing and giving us technologies which will make our present society look like the Dark Ages. God and the Masters will eventually win out, however, there is much resistance from greed, and unconsciousness of the Divine Mother, Goddess Energies, and the knowledge that Mother Earth is a living being!

Q: *What is the most important thing that Wesak offers to the planet at this time and how does participation in Wesak affect one's spiritual growth?*

A: I have been guided by the Masters to bring Wesak to the West on a global scale. To have an event with 2000 people from all over the world and all walks of life, overlighted by one million inner plane Ascended Masters, Angels, Elohim Masters and Christed Extraterrestrials under the Wesak full moon and the Mountain of Mt. Shasta, brings forth an astronomical amount of light, love and cleansing to this planet! Mt. Shasta, being one of the Earth's Chakras and such an incredible Spiritual Vortex, allows the Earth's Spiritual Grids to be lit up! Each year the Spiritual Current keeps building and it must be understood that Wesak in general is the high point of incoming Spiritual Energies to the Earth. It is also the holiest day of the year to the Ascended Masters. It is my honor to hold the Wesak Celebrations in Mt. Shasta, and it has become the most powerful event on this planet at this time. It also embodies synthesis, integration, and group consciousness! It is an event which allows all the Masters of all paths on Earth and in Heaven to be involved! Lord Buddha told me personally that he could not be more pleased with the event other than he and the Masters materializing on Earth and doing one themselves. I took this as a very kind and gracious compliment from him!

Q: *It is said that energy clearing sessions, etc. are provided by the Academy. Cannot one do this directly within one's own meditation contacts with one's Spiritual Guides and the Ascended Masters, or are the sessions provided by the Academy more effective? Are the services offered by the Academy making some people more dependent on an outside source instead of relying on their Self?*

A: One can definitely do clearing on oneself and that is what we teach. However, working with Spiritual Masters who are trained in this work can do it more quickly, deeper, and more effectively!

Q: *How would you describe your own relationship to Extraterrestrial life?*

A: Our connection to Extraterrestrials is being totally hidden by the governments of this world. It is the greatest cover-up in the history of the Earth. We have been contacted by over 100 species. We have over 20 different types of physical bodies in our possession from crashes on Earth. The United States government has actually been working with the Grays in underground bases. The United States government is testing all kinds of UFO technology! The world's governments are too war-like to allow the Christed Extraterrestrials to land and to allow us to be part of a Galactic government, as they truly would like us to be! In truth, this world has not left the Dark Ages yet. Even Atlantis was far more advanced than our present civilization. We are on the verge of a breakthrough in the next 12 to 40 years!

Q: *How do you see the role of Indigo Children?*

A: Indigo Children will have an enormous effect on our world. They are extremely advanced souls that have been incarnating during the last 20 to 30 years! They often have abilities far beyond anything we can conceive! They will be the hope of the future!

Q: *How do you understand "time" and "present moment" and their influence on our happiness?*

A: One can live in time and transcend negative ego. Why incarnate if this were not the case! Time has nothing to do with negative ego; it is how one uses time. It can be used by the negative ego in terms of always worrying or living in guilt, or one can live in the present with healthy planning for the future and appropriate enjoyment of the past!

Q: *Please comment on future "career" choices after our "earth school" is completed, as given in the Alice Bailey material.*

I have written about this in my book *Beyond Ascension*! Each person has seven career choices in which he or she can follow! I have gone into greater depth explaining these in *Beyond Ascension*!

Q: *Would you tell us what or who has been the greatest inspiration to your work?*

A: In terms of who or what has most inspired me, that is God! Second to God is the Ascended Masters, Archangels and Angels, Elohim Masters and Christed Extraterrestrials. I feel very connected to all these groups, however, I work very closely with the Ascended Masters, and they have told me that I am kind of like their point man on Earth! Being on the front lines, so to speak, is not always the easiest job, however, I love it. The examples and teachings of all the Masters of all religions, all Spiritual Paths, all Mystery Schools, and all paths to God have been my inspiration! God and my Spiritual path are my only interests in life and the only reason I am here is to be of service!

Warmest Regards and Love,
Dr Joshua David Stone

✶ ✶

64

"There is No Security Anymore"

Dear Dr. Stone:

As you might have heard, the universe decided to kick me out of my well-paid job some days ago and so I finally do not find any excuses anymore to proceed and develop teaching, healing, and organizing things in the spiritual realms on a deeper personal level.

Thank you for your words, I definitely do not have an easy time right now and having decided to let go of these kinds of work and to focus on teaching, healing, etc., sometimes scares me more than anything else in my life before. To allow that every day is a new day and that there is no security anymore, the only thing that helps is staying connected with my heart. The Masters are doing a great job with me and I appreciate their support, presence, and guidance.

It is really good to know that you are out there too.

Much Love

Dr. Stone's Reply:

GREETINGS MY FRIEND!

CONGRATULATIONS! SOMETIMES GOD AND THE MASTERS GIVE LIGHTWORKERS A LITTLE PUSH OUT OF THEIR COMFORTABLE NEST. A BLESSING IN DISGUISE!

I HAVE FOUR PIECES OF GUIDANCE FOR YOU:
WHY WORRY WHEN YOU CAN PRAY!
GOD AND THE MASTERS, YOUR PERSONAL POWER, THE POWER OF YOUR SUBCONSCIOUS MIND, AND YOUR PHYSICAL BODY ARE AN UNBEATABLE TEAM!
IF GOD AND THE MASTERS ARE FOR YOU, WHO OR WHAT CAN BE AGAINST YOU!
THE FORCE IS WITH YOU!

WARMEST REGARDS AND LOVE,
DR JOSHUA DAVID STONE

* *

65

"Dr. Stone, I am ready for your book now!"

Hello Dr. Stone,

I just received your two books. I have started *Soul Psychology*. Pretty darn good. I have been searching for this for five years. I had to go through my processes, but now I am ready for your material. I am so hungry for this, you have no idea. It makes me cry because I get so much joy from reading the truth and knowing that I am on the right path. It is totally beyond my comprehension, yet I understand. Thank you so much, Dr. Stone. I am so excited. It blows my mind how much literature you have written. I wish I were a speed-reader. I have been doing a lot of studying online, and I needed it all to pre-pare me for your literature. What is interesting to me is that 13 years of being a born again Christian during marriage, 10 years ago, the scripture did not EVEN mean to me what I understand it to mean now. There are so many lost people. I want to help. I crave this. Thank you for this opportunity in my lifetime.

Eternally,

Dr. Stone's Reply:

GREETINGS!

THANKS FOR YOUR VERY SWEET EMAIL! SO PLEASED YOU ARE ENJOYING *SOUL PSYCHOLOGY*! I KNEW YOU WOULD. WAIT UNTIL YOU READ *HOW TO RELEASE FEAR-BASED THINKING AND FEELING* AND *THE GOLDEN BOOK OF MELCHIZEDEK*. THOSE BOOKS WILL BLOW YOUR MIND! SO GLAD YOU ARE OPENING UP NOW! TAKE ADVANTAGE OF ALL THE SERVICES OF THE ACADEMY! COME TO THE IRI-DESCENT DIAMOND HEART WESAK! WORK WITH MY 15 AUDIO ASCENSION ACTIVATION TAPES. THE MASTERS AND I WANT TO PUT YOU ON THE FULL "ROCKETSHIP TO GOD" PROGRAM!

MUCH LOVE,
DR JOSHUA DAVID STONE

* *

66

"Do I continue with my Meditation?"

Dear Dr. Stone:

When I meditate in the morning, I sit about nine feet from a mirror. During meditation when I concentrate on my image, I see a second image of myself inside my image. This image is usually very clear and looks younger than me; sometimes it's larger than my actual reflection and sometimes smaller. During this, I also see my Heart Chakra clearly enclosed in a white energy circle plus some star-like lights on some other parts of my body. My question is: What is this? Should I continue this? Why does this happen?

Thank you.

Dr. Stone's Reply:

Greetings my Friend!

Thanks for your question! Yes, you should definitely continue your meditations as you are doing them. Your third eye is opening up and you are seeing the etheric body and subtle bodies transposed over the physical body! Study my Website to get trained in all this material so your Spirituality becomes integrated and balanced on a Spiritual, Psychological, and Physical/Earthly level! Work with some of the meditations on the Website as well! This is just the beginning! There is much more to come! Study the chapters on the Website as well! Read my books *The Complete Ascension Manual* and *Soul Psychology*! They will open your third eye even more!

Warmest Regards,
Dr Joshua David Stone

* *

67

Guidance regarding people run by the Negative Ego

GREETINGS!

IF YOU NEED SOME MONEY FOR FOOD LET ME KNOW. I WILL EXPRESS MAIL IT TO YOU. JUST SEND ME AN ADDRESS WHERE TO SEND IT!

I AM GLAD YOU ARE ENJOYING THE BOOKS. THESE ARE THE BOOKS OF BOOKS AS YOU SEE NOW, AND THERE ARE NO BETTER BOOKS TO GET YOU BACK ON TRACK!

IN TERMS OF WHAT IS GOING ON WITH YOUR FRIENDS, THIS HAS NOTHING TO DO WITH WHAT YOU ARE DOING. THIS JUST HAS TO DO WITH THESE PEOPLE BEING AT A VERY LOW STATE OF CONSCIOUSNESS AND BEING RUN BY THE NEGATIVE EGO. THE AREN'T BAD PEOPLE, THEY JUST DON'T KNOW WHAT THE NEGATIVE EGO IS SO IT RUNS THEM. IT IS GOOD THAT YOU HEALED THINGS WITH THEM

BUT THE LESSON IS YOU CANNOT TRUST THEM AND THEY CANNOT BE COUNTED ON. IT IS NOTHING YOU ARE DOING. IT IS NOT ANY PERSONAL KARMA. YOU MUST UNDERSTAND THAT WHEN YOU INCARNATE ONTO A PLANET YOU BUMP INTO OTHER PEOPLE'S LESSONS. NOT ALL KARMA IS PERSONAL IN THE SENSE THAT YOU DID SOMETHING TO CREATE THIS. YOU ARE NOT DOING ANYTHING AT ALL. THE LESSON IS TO DETACH FROM THESE PEOPLE!

EVERYTHING THAT HAPPENS IN YOUR LIFE IS FOR YOUR SOUL'S EVOLUTION, EVEN IF YOU DID NOT PERSONALLY SET THE KARMA IN MOTION BY ANYTHING YOU DID. SO JUST USE IT FOR SOUL GROWTH AND FORGIVE, BUT NO, THEY ARE NOT AT A LEVEL TO CONTROL THEIR EMOTIONAL BODIES OR NEGATIVE EGOS. YOU CAN TELL THEIR LEVEL OF CONSCIOUSNESS BY WHAT THEY ARE DOING. STALKING, GROUP SEX, PROMISING AND THEN NOT CALLING BACK. RUDENESS AND ARROGANCE ARE ALL SIGNS OF LOWER-SELF CONSCIOUSNESS RUNNING THESE PEOPLE. THEY ARE NOT EVIL; THEY ARE JUST RUN BY THE LOWER-SELF. THESE ARE NOT THE KINDS OF PEOPLE YOU CAN COUNT ON, EVEN IF THEY TRY TO MEAN WELL.

IN TERMS OF DEPRESSION, THIS IS CAUSED BY THE ATTITUDE OF GIVING UP. I KNOW IT IS HARD, BUT REMEMBER THAT EVERYTHING THAT HAPPENS IN LIFE IS POSITIVE AND A GIFT. EVEN WHAT IS GOING ON WITH YOU NOW! AGAIN, IT IS YOUR JOB INITIATION—EVERYTHING IS STRIPPED AWAY AND ALL THAT IS LEFT IS GOD! PUT YOUR FAITH IN GOD AND THE MASTERS. AGAIN, AT TIMES LIKE THIS YOU SEE WHO YOUR TRUE FRIENDS ARE! CALL ON GOD AND THE MASTERS. THE DEPRESSION IS A SIGN OF GIVING UP IN

YOUR ATTITUDE AND LOSING YOUR PERSONAL POWER AND
FIGHTING SPIRIT. THE KEY TO LIFE IS OWNING YOUR 100%
PERSONAL POWER AT ALL TIMES, BEING A SPIRITUAL WAR-
RIOR, HAVING A POSITIVE ATTITUDE, LOOKING AT EVERY-
THING AS A SPIRITUAL TEST AND LESSON, AND, AS YOU
SAID, HAVING PREFERENCES NOT ATTACHMENTS. IF IT IS
TRULY A PREFERENCE, THEN YOU ARE HAPPY EITHER WAY!
PRAY CONSTANTLY TO GOD, CHRIST, THE HOLY SPIRIT AND
THE MASTERS OF YOUR CHOICE! THE COMBINATION OF
YOUR SELF-MASTERY AND GOD, THE MASTERS', AND
ANGELS' HELP WILL PREVAIL.

SAY "NAKED I COME FROM MY MOTHER'S WOMB AND
NAKED SHALL I LEAVE! THE LORD GIVETH AND THE LORD
TAKETH AWAY. BLESSED BE THE NAME OF THE LORD!"

GOD AND THE MASTERS WILL SHOW YOU A WAY OUT OF
THIS IF YOU KEEP YOUR PERSONAL POWER, POSITIVE ATTI-
TUDE, SPIRITUAL WARRIOR SPIRIT, AND IF YOU KEEP YOUR
FAITH, TRUST AND PATIENCE. I WILL NOT LET YOU STARVE.
DO NOT BE AFRAID TO ACCEPT MY HELP IF YOU NEED IT.
YOU WOULD DO THE SAME FOR ME IF IT WERE REVERSED!
YOU WILL HAVE THE OPPORTUNITY TO HELP OTHERS IN
THE FUTURE! KEEP STUDYING THE BOOKS. TAKE EVERY
ACTION THE HOLY SPIRIT GUIDES YOU TO DO. GOD WILL
CREATE A MIRACLE ON YOUR BEHALF IF YOU DO AS I SAY! I
AM PUTTING YOU ON THE PRAYER ALTAR AGAIN AS WELL.

IF GOD BE FOR YOU, WHO OR WHAT CAN BE AGAINST YOU?
GOD KNOWS YOU ARE TRYING, AND RIGHTEOUSNESS IN
THE EYES OF GOD IS TRYING! GOD AND THE MASTERS WILL

NOT FAIL YOU. PUT YOUR TOTAL FAITH AND TRUST IN GOD
AND THE MASTERS AND WATCH A MIRACLE UNFOLD!

KODOISH, KODOISH, KODOISH, ADONAI TSABAYOTH
HOLY, HOLY, HOLY IS THE LORD GOD OF HOSTS!

WARMEST REGARDS AND LOVE,
DR JOSHUA DAVID STONE

* *

68

On Sins and Forgiveness

Dear Dr. Stone:

Hari Om Respected Sir,

What if a person has done some sins from which he was trying to come out of honestly and succeeded finally by praying to God. However, after getting rid of those sins he is punished for those sins by the society?

Thanking you, with love.

Dr. Stone's Reply:

Greetings my friend!

This is a very interesting question, which no one has asked me before! First, it is very good that you or the person you are speaking about has Spiritually changed their ways. God is by nature 100% loving and forgiving, as we should be to ourselves, and always welcomes his prodigal Sons and Daughters home no matter what their sins are. Mistakes are part of life and they should be learned from. As Christ said, "He that hath no sin, cast the first stone"! We have all made mistakes. As Yogananda said, "A sinner is a saint that never gave up"! So, the changes that have been made are duly noted by God and this is no small thing, so rejoice in this. Now, if after this Spiritual change has occurred karma still must be paid on the Earthly level then the lesson is to accept this with grace. You should say, "Not my will but thine, oh Lord, thank you for the lesson!" Pay your karmic debt with acceptance and a positive attitude. Do not give in to anger or depression! Society is a part of God as well, my friend, and if this has happened then God has played a part in it for God is not separate from society! Society is part of God as well! If you would like to be released from this earthly Karma then pray to God and the Masters for this. If it is meant to be it will happen. If it does not change then that means it is meant to be and it is your job to accept it with a positive attitude. The lesson in life is to bless everything that happens in life, for everything that happens in life is a Spiritual Test and Lesson. The lesson is to have only preferences not attachments. Things may not always go the way you want and the lesson is to be happy anyway and surrender to God's Will in all things; not the negative ego's will or the little will of the personality. It is okay to have preferences; however, you must surrender to God's Will in all things. Taking this attitude will bring you the peace of mind you seek in this situation and is the way God would have you interpret this situation, my friend! Study the free articles on my Website and this will train you to see life only through God's eyes and perspective!

Warmest Regards and love,
Dr Joshua David Stone

* *

69

"What is this High-Pitched Sound I Hear?"

Dear Dr Stone,

Early last year I saw your Website. I've been to the last two Wesaks and I'm looking forward to the next one. I have been slowly changing my life for the better ever since. Something's been happening to me for so long but no one else besides my husband knows what I'm talking about. I hope he's not just humoring me. He says he hears it too. A couple of times a week or so I hear these high-pitched sounds in my head. They usually last 1-5 seconds, sometimes up to 15, and then they're gone. It does not sound like it originates outside my head. Then, the other day, I heard the sound begin and I felt something pass from one ear across to the other through the middle of my head. It was a very distinct feeling that I have never felt before. I have been hearing these high-pitched noises for so many years that I have always ignored them but now I really want to know what they are. It is a perfectly even sound, like a machine made it. It reminds me of the hearing tests we got in elementary school. They put earphones on your head and you point your finger up when you hear a sound. They would start at a low frequency, make a one-second sound, go up in frequency slightly, make another one-second sound, and so on. That's the closest thing I can think of to what it sounds like. Like I said, this has happened so many times that I can't even think of when it started. But now I'm learning about a whole new world besides the physical and I wonder if there is an explanation for this. A few years ago I remember looking at a Website talking about alien implants and it mentioned certain sounds you might hear. At the time I thought it was nuts, but since I've changed and learned new things it doesn't sound nutty at all. It didn't really describe the sounds though. Do you know what I mean and where I can learn more? Whenever I start to hear one I stop whatever I'm doing and listen to it. Recently, I told my husband about it and he says he hears them too. Now whenever I hear one I turn to him and ask if he can hear it. About half the time he says he's hearing one too. Also, is this common? Help!

Sincerely,

Dr. Stone's Reply:

Greetings my friend!

The high-pitched sound I get as well sometimes. It is a subtle level of your clairaudience opening up. Sometimes it is the Masters' communication you are hearing. Sometimes it is certain Light Technologies that have been anchored to help in your clearing by the Masters and you are hearing the sound of the fifth-dimensional clearing devices at work! This was all set up by coming to Wesak!

Much Love,
Dr Joshua David Stone

* *

70

"What Planet is Djwhal Khul on?"

Dear Dr. Stone:

Can you tell me which planet Djwhal Khul is on?

Mucho Amor,

Dr. Stone's Reply:

Greetings!

He is not on any planet. He has transcended the material realm of existence and runs an inner plane ashram with Master Kuthumi and Lord Maitreya!

Much Love,
Dr Joshua David Stone

* *

71

"How Do I Deal With My Temper?"

Dear Dr. Stone:

I am very short tempered. Because of this I get angry very fast and loose control and say certain things to/about people which normally I won't say. I have strained relationships in the workplace due to this. How do I practically control my temper? How do I make up with the people who are hurt, who otherwise I like? This is also affecting my health. I feel fearful and anxious.

Regards,

Dr. Stone's Reply:

Greetings my Friend!

It is good you have asked this question! It is a sign that your soul is waking up! Anger is not of God! It is a manifestation of the lower-self mind. The exact definition of anger is "a loss of control and attempt to regain it." It is a sign of loss of self-mastery over your mind and emotions. This is not a judgment, just a lesson to learn that you are now ready to do. Your thinking causes all feelings and emotions. The thoughts that cause anger are attachment to people and things rather than having preference attitudes. Secondly, they are caused by not looking at everything in life as lessons and Spiritual tests. Thirdly, it is caused by not keeping up your bubble of protection and letting other people's negative energy victimize you. Lastly, it is caused by thinking from the negative ego/fear-based/separative/lower-self mind rather than thinking from your Spiritual/Christ/Buddha/Higher Self mind. You need to study my Website and read my book *Soul Psychology* and this will train you more completely on how to do this. Spirit and the Masters wish to congratulate you on your decision to awaken to your soul and claim your self-mastery over your energies now!

Warmest regards,
Dr Joshua David Stone

✳ ✳

72

"What is the Difference between Asking the Unconscious for Guidance or Praying to God?"

Dear Dr. Stone:

After several weeks of counseling, I had a wonderful healing when I finally reached and connected with that vast sea of the unconscious (yes, it really was!). Such a power, and the energy flowed through me with healing grace. I am aware it is my "servant" and waiting to help me in so many ways.

My question is, "What is the difference between asking the unconscious for guidance (it must hold a vastness of wisdom and experience!) and praying to God and the Masters? I know the Huna teachings talk of the upper, middle, and lower, and of course ultimately they must all be one. Is the unconscious a "personal" one or a collective, and does God indeed speak to us through that?

This leads onto a second quite complex question. A friend and I were in hot debate about the difference between calling in from above (soul colors, etc.) and going within to connect to the Divine. I feel that once one reaches the true within then the outer becomes that and it is really all one, but I guess it takes time to bring the two together. I seem to remember Hermes Trismegistus talking of this— that the inner becomes the outer.

Maybe I just think too much! Thank you dear one.

Dr. Stone's Reply:

Greetings!

Yes, there is an enormous difference between calling on the Higher Self, Mighty I AM Presence, and the Unconscious. The Unconscious has no reasoning. It can be communicated with by using a pendulum for very simple things relating to the personal self and body but that is about it. Ask for guidance from the Higher Self!

To call within or above is really the same thing! Two different ways of saying the same thing. No disagreement here!

Much Love,
Dr Joshua David Stone

* *

73

"Chapter Four of Soul Psychology always puts me on track!"

Super-electric Greetings Dr. Stone,

This is just another one of my shares. Chapter Four of the green *Soul Psychology* absolutely rocks…every time I allow insanity, despair, depression, anger, and/or self-pity to creep into my consciousness I read that chapter (I read it often)…and boom…I am kicked in the absolutely appropriate body part… back on track!

Just got an e-mail from a friend, of course I turned her on to the book and she advised me to re-read Chapter Four. I have never shared with her my love of Chapter Four and that I read it all the time, so cheers to Chapter Four!

Much love,

Dr. Stone's Reply:

GREETINGS!

THANKS FOR THE SWEET NOTE! I HAD TO CHECK AND SEE WHAT CHAPTER FOUR WAS, I FORGOT. LET ME TELL YOU SOMETHING. IF YOU LIKED CHAPTER FOUR THEN READ MY BOOKS *HOW TO RELEASE FEAR-BASED THINKING AND FEELING* AND *THE GOLDEN BOOK OF MELCHIZEDEK: HOW TO BECOME AN INTEGRATED CHRIST/BUDDHA IN THIS LIFETIME*! THIS IS 1400 PAGES OF CHAPTER FOUR, AND I AM NOT KIDDING. I AM LIKE E. F. HUTTON! WHEN I TELL YOU SOMETHING LIKE THIS, I DELIVER! CHECK IT OUT! IT WILL BLOW YOUR MIND!

THANKS AGAIN!

MUCH LOVE,
DR JOSHUA DAVID STONE

* *

74

"At what Initiation do we develop Higher Powers?"

Dear Dr. Stone,

I have a question for you. At what initiation do you start taking on and developing "Higher" powers of teleportation and psychic abilities? I have had a little heightening in my psychic abilities and a lot of improvement in intuition. I was just wondering—I would like to be able to instantly heal individuals by thought—don't know if it is really possible. I prefer to use those higher abilities to help others. In other words, when do you start taking on Ascended Master capabilities?

Since we last talked I joined Lord Maitreya's inner ashram leadership group, but I have had almost no contact that I can remember with such a group. Is there anything I can do to kick-start the situation?

Dr. Stone's Reply:

Greetings my friend!

Spiritual gifts such as teleportation and psychic abilities are not automatically connected to any particular initiation. They come as a product of your development, how you are constructed, and the grace of God! No level of initiation will guarantee you any specific ability!

Warmest regards,
Dr Joshua David Stone

* *

75

On the Challenge of Manifesting a Loving Relationship

Dear Dr. Stone:

Once more I need your clarity to help me undo some tangles!

I am still trying to understand some deep concepts—the more I try the more confused I'm becoming!

Firstly, I'll illustrate this by a little story. Surprisingly, I've never, ever experienced a loving relationship! Sounds unbelievable, but true. Not from parents, husband, daughter, or sister—even lovers!! So there's something wrong here. For the last 12 years I've attempted to manifest this (plus an income) all to no avail! It's not that I can't receive, but I believe it to be that I don't understand. To my mind, from that which I've read, need creates fear (that it won't be), anger if not manifest—that's the basic understanding. I become confused because the fact that I want to create something must mean that I'm attached to it! Surely I will become disappointed if it's not manifest because I if I expect it to, "expectations bring disappointments!" Conversely, I must expect a Miracle!! What a muddle!

So here I am really feeling that I can't have what I want/need, etc., and am going around in circles.

HELP!!!

Much love,

Dr. Stone's Reply:

Greetings!

It is very simple. Preference versus attachment. It is okay to have preferences. They are like wants, not needs. If they don't happen you are still happy, no disappointment and no anger! Expectations are attachments. Better to say hence, "I have a preference for a miracle." Or, have *expectancy* but not expectation! Go after your preferences with all your heart and soul and mind and might but remain happy until they happen!

Much Love,
Dr Joshua David Stone

* *

76

On Homosexuality

Dear Dr. Stone:

I'm looking for some written material about homosexuality. All I could find was a small chapter in your book on Romantic Relationships. I heard something (about homosexuality) that does not leave me comfortable, and whenever I feel so I start searching for more information about the matter in reference.

What I heard is what follows:

A very sensitive woman in my group told me she always sees bats flying around the head of homosexual people, and that those people are kind of being controlled by entities from the astral plane. It would be like a very heavy karma and to escape from that control is very difficult. The entities see homosexuals as their servers or slaves.

I think this "point of view" is very dangerous and quite prejudiced. It carries the prejudice that being homosexual is not natural or is wrong and that homosexuals should be helped to get free.

Your turn…

Love & Light,

Dr. Stone's Reply:

Greetings!

Thanks for your email. My friend, what this woman says about seeing bats flying around is ludicrous. What she is seeing is her own negative ego and faulty beliefs about homosexuality. Understand that clairvoyance is 100% colored by one's belief systems and consciousness. There is absolutely nothing wrong with homosexuality and it is not controlled by astral forces or entities any more than heterosexual relationships are. Do not buy into this illusion. It is negative ego glamour and maya! No judgment, but the woman's consciousness is not very developed or she is looking at a very small sample of subjects! Be clear on this point!

Much Love,
Dr. Joshua David Stone

* *

77

On the Hollow Earth and the Antichrist

Dear Dr. Stone:

What are your opinions of the Hollow Earth? Some say there is a passage to the Hollow Earth right beneath Mt. Shasta. What are your opinions of the antichrist? He will be taking the throne within years if humanity doesn't change soon. In fact, many people thinking they're doing good will actually set the lord of the world up. Any opinions or thoughts would be appreciated.

Dr. Stone's Reply:

Greetings my friend!

I would be happy to answer your questions. The Hollow Earth is real! It exists! The main entrances are at the North and South Poles. Under Mt. Shasta is an underground civilization called Telos. It is connected with all the underground cities of the world! They refer to us as the "surface dwellers"! You might enjoy reading my book *Hidden Mysteries*, for I have a chapter on the Hollow Earth!

In terms of the antichrist, this is real in a collective and individual sense. The force of the negative ego/fear-based/separative/lower-self/selfish mind which, of course, is the opposite of the Spiritual/Christ/Buddha Consciousness, is the cause of this. What you say is true; "the path to hell is paved with good intentions." Most of the people of the Earth are run by the negative ego and are totally unaware. This is not meant as a judgment, just a Spiritual discernment. It is not really their fault, they just have not been trained properly Spiritually and Psychologically. This includes a great many of the Spiritual Leaders as well. They are some of the most unconscious. One must be balanced and integrated Spiritually, Psychologically, and on a Physical/Earthly level! Your insights and keen and accurate!

Warmest Regards,
Dr Joshua David Stone

* *

78

On Evolution and Suffering

Dear Dr. Stone:

There are a couple of questions I'd like to ask you. One is about evolution; the other is about suffering. The one about evolution: I read your book and I believe that an animal becomes human by passing the portal, but I thought can God create a man without passing from animal to human? Like Adam Kadmon?

About suffering: I read a lot of people that say that you cannot deny your suffering, you have to recognize and accept it and that's one of the most important lessons you should know. I agree, but how can I do this? By facing the situations instead of running away from them, accepting my karma, my missions and this kind of stuff? Or is there anything else I could do?

I am God, you are God, everything is God, and I am this, but there is also hate, murders… God is not this, but is it because that people don't recognize they are God that they don't taste love? Well that's what I think.

A big hug from your friend,

Dr. Stone's Reply:

GREETINGS MY FRIEND!

IN REGARD TO EVOLUTION, THIS IS AN INTERESTING QUES-
TION. GOD INDEED CREATED PEOPLE OR SOULS, THAT IS A
FACT. THERE IS NO SUCH THING AS TRANSMIGRATION OF THE
SOUL. HOWEVER, ON A MONADIC LEVEL, THE MONAD HAS
HAD ASPECTS OF ITSELF IN THE MINERAL, PLANT AND ANI-
MAL KINGDOM. THIS IS NOT JUST MY GUIDANCE; THIS IS CON-
FIRMED IN THE WRITINGS OF DJWHAL KHUL IN THE ALICE
BAILEY BOOKS AND IN THE EDGAR CAYCE CHANNELINGS.

IN REGARD TO SUFFERING, YOUR THOUGHTS CREATE YOUR
REALITY. LORD BUDDHA CONFIRMED THIS IN HIS WRIT-
INGS OF THE FOUR NOBLE TRUTHS. HE SAID ALL SUFFER-
ING COMES FROM ATTACHMENT AND ALL SUFFERING
COMES FROM WRONG POINTS OF VIEW!

SO, MY SWEET FRIEND, YOU HAVE A LITTLE BIT OF FAULTY
THINKING ON THIS POINT, WITH NO JUDGMENT
INTENDED. THINGS ARE ONLY NEGATIVE IF YOU INTERPRET
THEM THAT WAY. IN TRUTH, ALL THINGS ARE JUST SPIRI-
TUAL TESTS AND LESSONS. EVERYTHING HAPPENS FOR A
REASON. IT IS POSSIBLE TO BE HAPPY UNDER ALL CIRCUM-
STANCES IF YOU HAVE PREFERENCES RATHER THAN
ATTACHMENTS. THE PHYSICAL BODY CAN SUFFER, HOW-
EVER, YOUR MIND AND EMOTIONS SUFFER ONLY IF YOU
INTERPRET LIFE FROM THE FROM THE NEGATIVE
EGO/FEAR-BASED/SEPARATIVE MIND'S PERSPECTIVE. THE

PROPER ATTITUDE TOWARDS ALL THINGS IN LIFE IS "NOT MY WILL BUT THINE, THANK YOU FOR THE LESSONS"! THE IDEAL IS TO WELCOME ADVERSITY, AS SAI BABA SAYS. THE IDEAL ATTITUDE, AS LORD BUDDHA SAYS, IS TO BLESS ALL THINGS. ALL ARE LESSONS IN FORGIVENESS AND UNCONDITIONAL LOVE!

WHEN JESUS WAS ON THE CROSS HIS PHYSICAL BODY MY HAVE SUFFERED BUT HIS SPIRIT, MIND AND BODY DID NOT. THIS IS WHY KRISHNA AND SAI BABA SAID THAT TO TRANSCEND DUALITY, WHETHER YOU HAVE PROFIT OR LOSS, PLEASURE OR PAIN, SICKNESS OR HEALTH, VICTORY OR DEFEAT, PRAISE OR CRITICISM, REMAIN THE SAME! EVERYTHING MUST BE PLACED ON THE ALTAR OF GOD! IT IS YOUR MIND THAT CREATES BONDAGE OR YOUR MIND THAT CREATES LIBERATION, AS SAI BABA HAS SAID. WHERE ONE PERSON PERCEIVES SOMETHING AS NEGATIVE, ANOTHER BLESSES IT AND THANKS GOD FOR IT AND ACCEPTS IT. ONE CAN LIVE IN ANGER OR UPSET OR DEPRESSION, OR IN ACCEPTANCE. IT IS YOUR THOUGHTS THAT CREATE YOUR FEELINGS AND EMOTIONS, NOT OUTSIDE SITUATIONS OR YOUR PHYSICAL BODY. ONE PERSON LOOKS AT SICKNESS OR ILLNESS AS A NEGATIVE AND ANOTHER PERSON LOOKS AT THEM AS SPIRITUAL TESTS, LESSONS, GIFTS, OPPORTUNITIES TO GROW, AND OPPORTUNITIES TO LEARN. IT IS YOUR PERSPECTIVE.

JESUS' BODY MAY HAVE SUFFERED, BUT JESUS' CONSCIOUSNESS DID NOT! THAT WAS HIS SPIRITUAL TEST, AND WHAT DID HE SAY, "FORGIVE THEM FATHER, FOR THEY KNOW NOT WHAT THEY DO"! THIS WAS JESUS' SUPREME SPIRITUAL TEST AND HE PASSED IT PERFECTLY. HE DEMONSTRATED THAT HE

COULD REMAIN IN THE CHRIST CONSCIOUSNESS, UNCON-
DITIONAL LOVE, AND INNER PEACE EVEN IF PHYSICALLY
KILLED. I AM NOT SAYING HE MAY NOT HAVE HAD TRYING
MOMENTS KNOWING THAT THIS LESSON WAS COMING.
CONCERN IS DIFFERENT THAN WORRY. AS EDGAR CAYCE
SAID, "WHY WORRY WHEN YOU CAN PRAY?" CONCERN IS
JUST TRYING TO BE PREPARED FOR A LESSON, SO JESUS
NEVER LEFT THE CHRIST CONSCIOUSNESS AND DID NOT
SUFFER IN HIS CONSCIOUSNESS. HIS BODY MAY HAVE FELT
SOME PAIN, HOWEVER, IF LOOKED AT AS A SPIRITUAL TEST,
LESSON AND GIFT, AND AS AN OPPORTUNITY TO REMAIN
EVENMINDED IN SICKNESS OR HEALTH OR IF THE BODY
FEELS GOOD OR BAD, HIS CONSCIOUSNESS DID NOT SUFFER.
DO YOU THINK BUDDHA WAS WRONG WHEN HE SAID ALL
SUFFERING COMES FROM ATTACHMENT AND ALL SUFFER-
ING COMES FROM WRONG POINTS OF VIEW? IF THERE ARE
NO ACCIDENTS AND EVERYTHING HAPPENS FOR A REASON
AND THERE IS NO SUCH THING AS LUCK, FOR ALL IS CAUSE
AND EFFECT, AND ALL IS GOD, THEN ANYTHING THAT HAP-
PENS HAS A GOD REASON AND GOD CAUSE. WHATEVER YOU
EXPERIENCE IS FOR THE GLORY OF GOD!

I HOPE THIS ANSWER HELPS!

ON THE LAST QUESTION, YOU ARE MOST DEFINITELY COR-
RECT. THAT IS AN EXCELLENT INSIGHT. IT IS BECAUSE THEY
DON'T SEE EVERYONE AND EVERYTHING AS GOD. IF THEY
DID, HOW COULD GOD MISTREAT GOD? IT WOULD BE LIKE
YOUR RIGHT HAND DOESN'T LIKE YOUR LEFT HAND.
COULD ANYTHING BE MORE RIDICULOUS, WITH NO JUDG-
MENT INTENDED! EVERY ENCOUNTER IN LIFE WITH A PER-
SON, ANIMAL, PLANT, OR MINERAL IS A HOLY ENCOUNTER

OF AN INCARNATION OF GOD MEETING AN INCARNATION OF GOD AT A DIFFERENT LEVEL OF EVOLVEMENT. THE MINERAL, PLANT, AND ANIMAL KINGDOMS ARE OUR YOUNGER BROTHERS AND SISTERS! ALL BEINGS IN THE INFINITE UNIVERSE ARE JUST INCARNATIONS OF GOD AT DIFFERENT LEVELS OF EVOLVEMENT. ALL RETURN TO GOD! IS IT NOT INDEED INCREDIBLE, MY FRIEND!

WARMEST REGARDS AND LOVE,
DR JOSHUA DAVID STONE

* *

79

"What Do I Keep Doing Wrong?"

Dear Dr. Stone,

I will keep this brief. I know you are busy. I have written you before. You have helped me immensely. When my partner attempted suicide, you gave me prayers and suggestions. I have followed those, and her recovery and mine has been incredible.

I am currently studying your book *How to Release Fear-Based Thinking and Feeling*, as you suggested. As you know, my partner's primary diagnosis is "borderline personality disorder" (which is a stupid name if you ask me, it should be called "Hyper-Magnified Negative Ego Disease"). I try to do as you say—every morning I ask for the light of protection, say my morning prayers, and try to keep positive Christ thoughts all day long. Now that my partner has become more stabilized we have moved to a new spot in the healing process. We have been in numerous heated arguments in the past few weeks. In every argument I go in saying a prayer, vowing I will not go to the emotion/fear place, and every time she is able to draw out my fear-based negative ego. I end up becoming defensive, angry, and frustrated. I go to therapy so that I can continue to learn improved ways to communicate with her and stay clear with my issues. My question is this: after studying all of your work that I have so far, knowing what I know, why I do I keep reacting from the old place? I understand why I have the fears, but how do I keep from feeding myself into her fears (and mine for that matter). I get to these places and all of a sudden its like I never read anything, prayed, healed, or did anything positive. She can just push the buttons and I react. I know I must stay on the path I'm on and continue my studies but I could use a new tool right now, if you know what I mean. What do I keep doing incorrectly?

Thanks for your time.

Dr. Stone's Reply:

GREETINGS MY FRIEND!

I KNOW EXACTLY WHAT YOU SPEAK OF. YOU ARE NOT THE ONLY ONE THIS HAPPENS TO. THIS IS WHAT YOU NEED TO DO: EVERY MORNING GET UP AND SAY OUT LOUD AND/OR IN TYPING OR WRITING, A PERSONAL VOW TO SELF AND GOD AND THE MASTERS THAT THIS DAY YOU WILL HOLD TO YOUR CHRIST CONSCIOUSNESS IN RELATIONSHIP TO THIS PERSON AS YOUR NUMBER ONE PRIORITY IN LIFE. THEN PRAY TO GOD AND THE MASTERS FOR HELP IN JUST MASTERING THIS LESSON THIS DAY. DO THIS EVERY SINGLE DAY RELIGIOUSLY FOR ONE YEAR! THIS IS A SPIRITUAL TEST, AND THE REASON YOU CAN'T DO IT IS YOU HAVE NOT MADE UP YOUR MIND SUFFICIENTLY.

THEN ALL DAY LONG SAY TO YOU YOURSELF, "DO I WANT GOD OR DO I WANT MY NEGATIVE EGO?" PUT ON YOUR MENTAL AND SPIRITUAL ARMOR EVERY MORNING AND GET PREPARED TO BATTLE YOUR NEGATIVE EGO. KEEP A LOG AND TRY TO SEE HOW MANY DAYS YOU CAN GO WITH-OUT FIGHTING. IF YOU MAKE A MISTAKE, FORGIVE SELF, LEARN THE LESSON, AND REDOUBLE YOUR PERSONAL COMMITMENT. THIS WILL WORK FOR SURE. THIS IS WHAT I FINALLY HAD TO DO WITH MYSELF WITH EMOTIONALLY AND NEGATIVELY EGO-RUN PEOPLE WHO ARE AROUND ME CONSTANTLY AND CANNOT BE AVOIDED! LOOK AT IT AS THE SUPREME SPIRITUAL TEST OF YOUR LIFE. MAKE IT THE NUMBER ONE FIRST THING YOU DO EVERY MORNING AND IF NECESSARY SAY IT TEN TIMES A DAY OR 1000 TIMES A DAY IF NECESSARY UNTIL YOU MASTER THE LESSON. BLESS THIS PERSON FOR TEACHING YOU THIS LESSON. THE FORCE IS WITH YOU, MY FRIEND!

KEEP UP THE GOOD WORK. KEEP STUDYING THE BOOKS. READ *THE GOLDEN BOOK OF MELCHIZEDEK, HOW TO CLEAR THE NEGATIVE EGO*, AND *INTEGRATED ASCENSION*. THEY WILL GREATLY HELP AS WELL, AND GIVE YOU MORE ARTILLERY!

WARMEST REGARDS,
DR JOSHUA DAVID STONE

* *

80

The Soul and Mind are Separate from the Brain

Greetings!

Thanks for your email! I am so pleased you are enjoying *Soul Psychology* and are planning to read the other ones as well.

Yes. Personality disorders, the brain, mapping the mind. All interesting questions, my friend. Understand that the soul and mind are separate from the brain. One has the same problems when one dies and leaves the physical body and brain behind, which is proof of that. The mind affects the brain more than the brain affecting the mind.

It is your thoughts that create your reality, not your brain. Personality disorders are nothing more than faulty thinking patterns in different configurations. If people were taught to think properly personality disorders would all go away in an instant! They all stem from negative ego thinking in different combinations and permutations. Transcend negative ego/fear-based/separative/lower-self thinking and replace it with

Spiritual/Christ/Buddha/God consciousness, in an integrated and balanced manner, and personality disorders all instantly disappear. So, let this be your focus, my friend!

Much Love,
Dr Joshua David Stone

* *

81

Dr. Stone on Psychiatry and Medical Doctors

GREETINGS MY FRIEND!

THANKS FOR YOUR EMAIL. I AM SO PLEASED YOU ARE ENJOYING THE WEBSITE. YOUR IDEA ABOUT DOING WORK IN THE FIELD OF PSYCHIATRY AND SPIRITUAL AWAKENING IS MOST WONDERFUL. THIS IS NOT AN AREA VERY MANY PEOPLE SPEAK ABOUT VERY MUCH. YOU HAVE MOTIVATED ME, MY FRIEND, TO MAYBE DO SOME SERVICE WORK MYSELF IN THIS AREA.

THE NUMBER OF PEOPLE WHO ARE HAVING SPIRITUAL EXPERIENCES AND AWAKENING AND ARE BEING LABELED, BY PERSONALITY LEVEL SO-CALLED DOCTORS, IS ASTOUNDING. IN TRUTH, IN MANY WAYS WE ARE STILL LIVING IN THE DARK AGES. DOCTOR HEAL THYSELF. MORE OFTEN THAN NOT, THEY ARE DOING MORE DESTRUCTION THAN GOOD. AS YOU KNOW, MOST PSYCHIATRISTS ARE MEDICALLY

TRAINED AND NOT PSYCHOLOGICALLY OR SPIRITUALLY TRAINED. SO THEY THINK CHEMICALS IN THE BODY CREATE PEOPLE'S EXPERIENCE SO THEY TREAT IT WITH DRUGS. ON RARE OCCASIONS, IN SEVERE CASES, THIS COULD BE OF VALUE FOR A SHORT TIME. HOWEVER, FOR THE MOST PART THIS IS BARBARIC! SOME EVEN USE ELECTRIC SHOCK THERAPY. THE PILLS KILL THE SPIRITUAL EXPERIENCE, POISON THE PERSON, DRUGS THEM, AND THEY CALL THAT THERAPY. AT BEST, IF THE PATIENT IS LUCKY, THERE CAN BE SOME PERSONALITY-LEVEL THERAPY, BUT MOST PSYCHIATRISTS ARE NOT EVEN PROPERLY TRAINED IN THAT. THEY ARE MEDICAL DOCTORS AND USE A MEDICAL MODEL! THEY NOT ONLY DO NOT UNDERSTAND ANY SPIRITUAL REALITY; THEY DO NOT UNDERSTAND ANY PSYCHOLOGICAL ONE EITHER. SO ANY SERVICE WORK YOU CAN DO IN THIS AREA IS GREATLY NEEDED, MY FRIEND!

WARMEST REGARDS,
DR JOSHUA DAVID STONE

* *

82

"I Want to Pursue a Fuller Path of Spiritual Service

Dear Dr. Stone:

Greetings from my heart,

I feel strongly that I am being led to inquire and explore the possibilities of a future that includes facilitating spiritual counseling, and, hopefully, working through a branch of the Academy.

Currently I labor at my job, farm, and facilitate healing work. I am hoping to manifest a speedy retirement from my job that will allow me to pursue a fuller path of spiritual service.

Could you enlighten me as to how I may proceed?

Many thanks and blessings,

Dr. Stone's Reply:

Greetings my Friend!

The first step is to become fully integrated in the Academy's work. I would definitely recommend reading these other books of mine. I have actually now completed 31 volumes in my "Ascension Book Series," however, these are the ones I would recommend reading first. They are all available from the Academy.

Soul Psychology
How to Release Fear-Based Thinking and Feeling: An In-depth Study of Spiritual Psychology
The Golden Book of Melchizedek: How to Become an Integrated Christ/Buddha in This Lifetime
How to Clear the Negative Ego
Integrated Ascension
The Complete Ascension Manual
The Soul's Perspective on How to Achieve Perfect Radiant Health

Then get my 15 audio Ascension Activation Meditation Tapes and work with one tape a day, and on the seventh day rest. For the first 21 days, however, only listen to my tape called "The 18 Point Cosmic Cleansing Meditation"! This work will totally cleanse and spiritually electrify your energy fields!

Then, if there is anyway possible that you can come to the "Iridescent Diamond Heart Wesak," this would completely transform your consciousness and being! I call this three-part program the "Rocketship to GOD." Trust in this work, for it is the answer you seek and Spirit and the Masters have guided you to it!

The combination of the books, the Ascension Activation Meditation Tapes, studying the Website, getting some channeled sessions with Wistancia for an initiation, ray reading and light quotient session, implant and negative elemental session, ascension clearing session, and with coming to the Diamond Heart Wesak, will put you on the "Rocketship to GOD"! You will be fully integrated then in the work and you will become a fully integrated Christ, achieve integrated ascension, and fully embody the work on Earth!

Then the possibility of opening a branch is a possibility doing ascension classes following my book, and so on. However, to be a full teacher and channel of the work you must fully integrate and embody the work. This is the first step! You can order all these products and set all this up through the Academy! Welcome to the team!

Much Love,
Dr Joshua David Stone

✷ ✷

83

"I Started on the Path and I want More!"

Dear Dr. Stone:

I have read a piece of your wife's literature on the Goddess Role of Manifestation. I found it very interesting. I have read your newcomers welcome note and have decided to order the first two books that you recommend.

I am on a tremendous spiritual journey, and the more knowledge that I get, the more I want. My daughter was killed in a car accident five years ago and this started me on my journey.

You give a lot of information that I am not familiar with, but I guess by reading your literature I will find it all out. If feel a tad susceptible because you are so knowledgeable and have so many followers, that it reminds me of episodes like Jim Jones. Not that I could possibly accuse you of anything, it is just my fears, I guess. I know the difference between good and bad.

Thank you for reading my email and for your wonderful service to the planet.

Sincerely,

Dr. Stone's Reply:

Greetings my Friend!

Thanks for your sweet note and sharing!

Your two books will go out today! Read *Soul Psychology* first. This book will blow your mind! It will bring you a peace that passeth understanding! The *Complete Ascension Manual* will open up a whole new world for you.

My sweet friend, you are being guided to my work now by Spirit and the Masters. It is the next step in your journey. I have a large global following; not because I am like Jim Jones, but because my books and teachings are, I very humbly tell you, some of the most advanced, cutting-edge, easy to understand, practical, integrated and synthesized teachings on the planet that are totally supported by Spirit and the Masters. The number of students does not necessarily equate to degrees of corruption, although in this world you may have a point! By the grace of GOD and the Masters, I do not fit into this category, however. When you are done with these two books, trust me, and read my book *How to Release Fear-Based Thinking and Feeling: An In-depth Study of Spiritual Psychology*. You will never be the same! These books are the premiere Ascended Master Teachings you will find on this planet!

When you are ready, work with my 15 audio Ascension Activation Meditation Tapes, which were created to work with the books. All this can be done in the comfort of your own home! Finding this work will accelerate your evolution literally 10,000-fold!

What is unique about this work is that it is cutting-edge—on a Spiritual, Psychological, and Physical/Earthly level—and is totally balanced and integrated. It is the most in-depth yet easy to understand training program and most effective you will find anywhere in the world. You are really in for a treat! Trust your intuition and feelings, and my words will echo and reverberate with truth throughout your being. Do not underestimate the profundity of this moment!

Warmest Regards,
Dr Joshua David Stone

My Spiritual Mission and Purpose
by Dr Joshua David Stone

My Spiritual mission and purpose is a multifaceted process. Spirit and the inner plane Ascended Masters have asked myself and Wistancia (married since 1998), to anchor onto the Earth an inner plane Ashram and Spiritual/Psychological/Physical/Earthly Teaching and Healing Academy! This Academy is called the Melchizedek Synthesis Light Academy! We are overlighted in this mission by Melchizedek, the Mahatma, Archangel Metatron, the Inner Plane Ascended Master Djwhal Khul, and a large group of Ascended Masters and Angels such as the Divine Mother, Archangel Michael, Archangel Gabriel, Sai Baba, Vywamus, the Lord of Arcturus, Lord Buddha, Lord Maitreya, Mother Mary, Quan Yin, El Morya, Kuthumi, Serapis Bey, Paul the Venetian, Master Hilarion, Sananda, Lady Portia and Saint Germain, and a great many others who we like to call the "Core Group"!

I have also been asked by the inner plane Ascended Master Djwhal Khul, who again wrote the Alice Bailey books, and was also involved in the Theosophical Movement, to take over his inner plane Ashram when he moves on to his next Cosmic Position, in the not too distant future.

Djwhal holds Spiritual Leadership over what is called the inner plane Second Ray Synthesis Ashram. On the inner plane the Second Ray Department is a gigantic three story building complex with vast gardens.

The Ascended Master Djwhal Khul runs the first floor of the Second Ray Department in the Spiritual Hierarchy. Master Kuthumi, the Chohan of the Second Ray, runs the second floor. Lord Maitreya the

Planetary Christ runs the third floor! When Djwhal Khul leaves for his next Cosmic Position, I will be taking over this first floor Department. The Second Ray Department is focused on the "Spiritual Education" of all lightworkers on Earth and is the Planetary Ray of the Love/Wisdom of God. What is unique, however, about the Synthesis Ashram is that it has a unique mission and purpose which is to help lightworkers perfectly master and integrate all 12 Planetary Rays which is one of the reasons I love this particular Spiritual leadership position and assignment so much! For this has been a great mission and focus of all my work!

Wistancia's and my mission has been to anchor the Synthesis Ashram and Teaching Academy onto the physical Earth, which we have done and are continuing to do in an ever increasing manner on a global level. Currently there are 40 branches of the Academy that have been set up around the world! The Academy actually first came into existence in 1996! This we have been guided to call the Melchizedek Synthesis Light Academy for the following reasons. It is called this because of the Overlighting Presence of Melchizedek (Our Universal Logos), the Mahatma (Avatar of Synthesis), and the Light which is the embodiment of Archangel Metatron, who created all outer light in our Universe and is the creator of the electron! These three beings, Djwhal Khul, and a very large Core Group of inner plane Planetary and Cosmic Masters help us in all this work.

I have also been asked by the inner plane Ascended Masters to be one of the main "High Priest Spokespersons for the Planetary Ascension Movement on Earth." I have been asked to do this because of the cutting-edge, yet easy to understand nature of all my books and work, as well as certain Spiritual Leadership qualities I humbly possess. In this regard, I represent all the Masters, which works out perfectly given the Synthesis nature of my work. I function as kind of a "Point Man" for the Ascended Masters on Earth, as they have described it to me.

The Masters, under the guidance of Lord Buddha our Planetary Logos, have also guided us as part of our mission to bring Wesak to the

West! So, for the last seven years we have held a Global Festival and Conference at Mt. Shasta, California for 2000 people. This, of course, honors the Wesak Festival, which is the holiest day of the year to the inner plane Ascended Masters, and the high point of incoming Spiritual energies to the Earth on the Taurus full moon each year! We invite all lightworkers to join us each year from all over the world for this momentous celebration, which is considered to be one of the premiere Spiritual Events in the New Age Movement!

The fourth part of my mission and purpose is the 40 volume "Easy to Read Encyclopedia of the Spiritual Path" that I have written. So far, I have completed 31 volumes in this Ascension Book Series. The Ascended Master Djwhal Khul prophesized in the 1940's that there would be a third dispensation of Ascended Master teachings what would appear at the turn of the century. The first dispensation of Ascended Master teachings was the Theosophical Movement, chan-neled by Madam Blavatsky. The second dispensation of Ascended Master teachings was the Alice Bailey books, channeled by Djwhal Khul, and *The I AM Discourses*, channeled by Saint Germain. My 40 volume series of books is by the grace of GOD and the Masters, the third dis-pensation of Ascended Master teachings as prophesized by Djwhal Khul. These books are co-creative channeled writings of myself and the inner plane Ascended Masters. What is unique about my work is how easy to read and understand it is, how practical, comprehensive, cut-ting-edge, as well as integrated and synthesized. Wistancia has added to this work with her wonderful book *Invocations to the Light*.

The fifth aspect of our work and mission, which is extremely unique, is the emphasis of "Synthesis." My books and all my work integrate in a very beautiful way all religions, all Spiritual paths, all mystery schools, all Spiritual teachings, and all forms of psychology! Everyone feels at home in this work because of its incredible inclusive nature! This syn-thesis ideal is also seen at the Wesak Celebrations, for people come from all religions, Spiritual paths, mystery schools, and teachings. The event is overlighted by over one million inner plane Ascended Masters, Archangels and Angels, Elohim Masters, and Christed Extraterrestrials. Wesak, the books, the Academy, and all our work embody this synthesis principle. This is part of why I and we have been given Spiritual Leadership of the Synthesis Ashram on Earth, and soon on the Inner Plane as well. This also explains our unique relationship to Melchizedek who holds responsibility for the "synthesis development" of all beings in our universe. Our connection to the Mahatma is explained by the fact that the Mahatma is the Cosmic embodiment of "synthesis" in the infinite Universe. This is also why the Mahatma also goes by the name, "The Avatar of Synthesis." Archangel Metatron who holds the position in the Cosmic Tree of Life of Kether, or the Crown, hence has a "Synthesis Overview" of all of the Sephiroth or Centers of the Cosmic Tree of Life! Djwhal Khul holds Spiritual leadership of the "Synthesis Ashram" on the Planetary, Solar, and Galactic levels for the Earth! The Core Group of Masters that overlight our mission are, again, the embodiment of the synthesis understanding!

The unique thing about our work is that it teaches some of the most cutting-edge co-created channeled work on the planet, in the realm of Ascension and Ascended Master Teachings. This can be seen in my books *The Complete Ascension Manual, Beyond Ascension, Cosmic Ascension, Revelations of a Melchizedek Initiate,* and *How to Teach Ascension Classes.* Because of my background as a Psychologist and licensed Marriage, Family and Child Counselor, I also specialize in some of the most advanced cutting-edge work on the planet in the field of Spiritual psychology. In this regard, I would guide you to my books, *Soul Psychology, Integrated Ascension, How to Clear the Negative Ego,* and *Ascension and Romantic Relationships!* Thirdly, I also have humbly brought forth some extremely cutting-edge work on the physical/earthly level in the field of healing, Spirituality and society, politics, social issues, Extraterrestrials, Spiritual leadership, Spirituality and business, Goddess work with Wistancia, and of course the annual Wesak Celebrations. This can be found in my books: *The Golden Keys to Ascension and Healing, Hidden Mysteries, Manual for Planetary Leadership, Your Ascension Mission: Embracing Your Puzzle Piece, How to be Successful in your Business from a Spiritual and Financial Perspective,* and *Empowerment and Integration Through The Goddess* —written by Wistancia and myself.

Adding to this, the 11 new books I have just completed and am completing: *The Golden Book of Melchizedek: How to Become an Integrated Christ/Buddha in this Lifetime, How to Release Fear-Based Thinking and Feeling: An In-depth Study of Spiritual Psychology, The Little Flame and Big Flame* (my first children's book), *Letters of Guidance to Students and Friends, Ascension Names and Terms Glossary, Ascension Activation Meditations of the Spiritual Hierarchy, The Divine Blueprint for the Seventh Golden Age, How to do Psychological and Spiritual Counseling for Self and Others, God and His Team of Super Heroes* (my second children's book) and *How to Achieve Perfect Radiant Health from the Soul's Perspective*!

Currently I have completed 31 volumes in my Ascension Book Series. Fourteen of these books are published by Light Technology Publishers. A newer version of *Soul Psychology* is published by Ballantine Publishers, owned by Random House, which I am quite excited about as well! The other books are in manuscript form and I am currently negotiating with various publishers for publishing rights! My books have also been translated and published in Germany, Brazil, Japan, Holland, Israel and this process continues to expand.

Spirit and the inner plane Ascended Masters have told me that because of this unique focus, that what I have actually done in a co-creative way and manner with them, is open a new Portal to God. This new portal opening stems out of all the cutting-edge Ascension Activations and Ascended Master Teachings, the totally cutting-edge Spiritual Psychology work because of my background as a Psychologist and licensed Marriage, Family and Child Counselor, and the unique ability to ground all the work into the physical/earthly world in a balanced and integrated manner. Spirit and the Masters have told me that this new

Portal to God is on an inner and outer plane level, and continues to be built in a co-creative way with Spirit, the Masters, myself, and certain other Masters and High Level Initiates who are helping me on the inner and outer planes! I have Spiritual leadership, however, in spearheading this project, and it is one of the most exciting projects I am involved in.

In terms of my Spiritual initiation process as I have spoken of in my books, I have currently now taken my 16th major initiation. These are not the minor initiations that some groups work with, but are the major initiations that embody all the minor initiations within them. The Seventh Initiation is the achieving of Liberation and Ascension. The 10th Initiation is the completion of Planetary Ascension and the beginning of Solar Initiation. The 11th Initiation, being the first Galactic Initiation. The 12th Initiation, being the first Universal Initiation from an Earthly perspective. Having taken my 16th initiation, what is most important to me is that these initiations have been taken in an "integrated manner," for, in truth, the Masters told me that they are not really into Ascension, which may surprise a great many lightworkers. The Masters are into "*Integrated* Ascension"! There are many lightworkers taking initiations, but many are not doing so in an integrated and balanced manner! They are taking them on a Spiritual level, but they are not being properly integrated into the mental and emotional bodies or psychological level properly. They are also not transcending negative ego/fear-based thinking and feeling, and properly balancing their four-body system. They are also not integrating their initiations fully into the Physical/Earthly level, addressing such things as: Healing, Grounding their Missions, Finding their Puzzle Piece Mission and Purpose, Prosperity Consciousness and Financial and Earthly Success, Integrating the God/Goddess, Embracing the Earth Mother and the Nature Kingdom, Properly Integrating into Third-Dimensional Society and Civilization in terms of the focus of their Service Mission. This is just mentioned as a very loving reminder of the importance of an integrated and balanced approach to one's Spiritual Path. The grace to have been able to take these 16 major initiations and be able to have completed my Planetary Ascension process and to have moved deeply into my Cosmic Ascension process, I give to GOD, Christ, the Holy Spirit, Melchizedek, the Mahatma, Archangel Metatron, and the Core Group of Masters I work with. I have dedicated myself and my life to GOD and the Masters' service, and I have humbly attempted to share everything I know, have used, and have done in my Spiritual path and Ascension process with all of you, my Beloved Readers!

Melchizedek, the Universal Logos, has also inwardly told me, that because of the Cosmic work I am involved with, that I have taken on the Spiritual assignment of being one of the "12 Prophets of Melchizedek on Earth." I am very humbled to serve in this capacity. For Melchizedek is the Universal Logos, who is like the President of our entire Universe. In truth, all Religions and Spiritual teachings have their source in Melchizedek and in the Great Ancient Order of Melchizedek. It is my great honor and privilege to serve GOD and Melchizedek in this capacity. This is something I have never spoken of before, although I have known of this for many, many years. I have been guided after all this time to share a little more deeply about my Spiritual mission on Earth at this time.

The Academy Website is one of the most profound Spiritual Websites you will ever explore because it embodies this "synthesis nature" and is an ever-expanding, living, easy-to-read Spiritual "encyclopedia" that fully integrates all 12 Rays in design and creation! This is also embodied in the free 140-page information packet that we send out to all who ask who wish to get involved and know more about our work! The information in the information packet is also available by just exploring the Academy Website!

We have also set up a wonderful Ministers Ordination and Training Program, which we invite all interested to read about. I am also very excited about a relatively recent book I have written called *How to Teach Ascension Classes*. Because I have become so busy with my Spiritual leadership and global world service work, I really do not have the time to teach weekly classes, as I have in the past. I firmly believe in the motto "Why *give* a person a fish, when you can *teach* them to fish!" In this vein, the Masters guided me to write a book on how to teach people to teach Ascension classes based on my work. I humbly suggest it is a most wonderful channeled book that can teach you in the easiest way and manner on every level to teach Ascension classes in your home or on a larger level if you choose. These classes are springing up now all over the globe and have been successful beyond my wildest dreams and expectations. When I wrote the book I was so involved with the process of writing it, I never fully envisioned the tremendous success it would have on a planetary and global level. Using this book and my other books, I have really done the initial homework for you, which can and will allow you to immediately begin teaching Ascension classes yourself. I humbly suggest that you look into the possibility of doing this yourself if you are so guided!

One other very interesting aspect of our Spiritual mission is something the Masters have been speaking to us about for over 10 years which is what they described as being "Ambassadors for the Christed Extraterrestrials"! We have always known this to be true! This was part of the reason I wrote the book *Hidden Mysteries*, which I humbly suggest is one of the best overviews in an easy to read and understand manner, of the entire Extraterrestrial Movement as it has affected our planet. If you have not read this book, I highly recommend that you do so. It is truly fascinating reading! My strongest personal connection to the Extraterrestrials is with the Arcturians! The Arcturians are the most advanced Christed Extraterrestrial race in our galaxy. They hold the future blueprint for the unfoldment of this planet. The Arcturians are like our future planet and future selves on a collective level. Part of my work, along with the Ascended Master Teachings I have been asked to bring through, has been to bring through a more conscious and personal connection to the Arcturians, the Ashtar Command, and other such Christed Extraterrestrial races. I also encourage you to read my book *Beyond Ascension* where I explore some of my personal experiences with the Arcturians, and how you may do so as well!

Currently, behind the scenes, we are working on some further expansions of this aspect of our mission, which we will share at a later time! Wistancia has also been involved with "White Time Healing," which is another most wonderful Extraterrestrial healing modality that she offers to the public!

One other aspect of our mission deals with having developed, with help from the inner plane Ascended Masters, some of the most advanced Ascension activation processes to accelerate Spiritual evolution that has ever been brought forth to this planet. In this co-creative process with the Masters, we have discovered the "keys" to how to accelerate Spiritual evolution at a rate of speed that in past years and centuries would have been unimaginable! This is why I call working with the Ascended Masters "The Rocketship to GOD Method of Spiritual Growth." There is no faster path to God Realization than working with the Ascended Masters, Archangels and Angels, Elohim Masters and Christed Extraterrestrials! What is wonderful about this process is that you do not have to leave your current Spiritual practice, religion, or Spiritual path. Stay on the path you are and just integrate this work into what you are currently doing! All paths as you know, lead to GOD, my friends! This is the profundity of following an eclectic path, and path of synthesis! I humbly suggest I have found some shortcuts! I share this with all lightworkers on earth, for I love GOD with all my heart and soul and mind and might, and I recognize that we are all incarnations of GOD, and Sons and Daughters of this same GOD, regardless of what religion, Spiritual path, or mystery school we are on. We are all, in truth, the Eternal Self and are all God! There is, in truth, only GOD, so what I share with you, I share with you, GOD, and myself for in the highest sense we are all one! What we each hold back from each other, we hold back from ourselves and from GOD. This is why I give freely all that I am, have learned and have, to you, my Beloved Readers, giving everything and holding back nothing! In my books and audiotapes, I have literally shared every single one of these ideas, tools, and Ascension activation methods for accelerating evolution that I have used and come to understand. My Beloved Readers, these tools and methods found in my books and on the audiotapes will "blow your mind as to their effectiveness," in terms of how profound, and easy to use they are! I would highly recommend that all lightworkers obtain the 13 Ascension Activation Meditation tapes I have put together for this purpose. Most of them were taped at the Wesak Celebrations with 1500 to 2000 people in attendance, with over one million inner plane Ascended Masters, Archangels and Angels, Elohim Masters, and Christed Extraterrestrials in attendance, under the Wesak full moon and the mountain of Mt Shasta. You can only imagine the power, love, and effectiveness of these Ascension activation audiotapes. I recommend getting all 13 tapes and working with one tape every day or every other day! I personally guarantee you that these tapes will accelerate your Spiritual evolution a thousandfold! You can find them in the information packets and on our Website. They are only available from the Academy! Trust me on this, the combination of reading my books, Wistancia's book, and working with these audio ascension activation tapes, will accelerate your Spiritual evolution beyond your wildest dreams and imagination!

One other extremely important part of my mission, which is a tremendous Spiritual passion of mine, is the training of lightworkers on earth in the area of Spiritual/Christ/Buddha thinking and negative ego/separative/fear-based thinking! These are the only two ways of thinking in the world, and each person thinks with one, the other, or a combination of both. If a person does not learn how to transcend negative ego thinking and feeling, it will end up, over time, corrupting every aspect of their lives including all channeling work, Spiritual teaching, and even healing work! One cannot be wrong with self and right with GOD. This is because our thoughts create our reality, as we all know! I cannot recommend more highly that every person reading this book, read my other books: *Soul Psychology, The Golden Book of Melchizedek: How to Become an Integrated Christ/Buddha in this Lifetime*, and *How to Release Fear-Based Thinking and Feeling: An In-depth Study of Spiritual Psychology*! I humbly suggest that these three books will be three of the most extraordinary self-help books in the area of mastering this psychological area of life. They are extremely easy to read, very practical and filled with tools that will help you in untold ways. Being a channel for the Ascended Masters and being uniquely trained as a Spiritual Psychologist and Marriage, Family and Child Counselor, as well as being raised in a family of psychologists, has given me an extraordinary ability to teach this material through my books in a most effective manner. The combination of my books on Ascension, and these books on Spiritual Psychology, along with Wistancia's book on the art of invocation, will literally revolutionize your consciousness in the comfort of your own home! The most extraordinary thing about all this work is how incredibly easy to read, and easy to understand it is. It is also incredibly comprehensive, completely cutting-edge, and total-ly integrated, balanced, and synthesized. It contains the best of all schools of thought in the past, present, and channeled cutting-edge future understanding that is available now! I humbly ask you to trust me in this regard and just read one of these books and you will imme-diately want to buy the others!

One other aspect of our work and mission is our involvement with the "Water of Life" and the Perfect Science products for the healing of our own physical bodies and the physical body of Mother Earth of all pollution in the air, water and earth. This is the miracle Mother Earth has been waiting for to bring her back to her "original edenic state" after so much abuse. This is not the time or the place to get into this subject in detail; however, I invite you to check out the "Water of Life" and the Perfect Science information in the Information Packet and on the Academy Website! It is truly the miracle we have all been waiting for to help heal the Earth!

One other aspect of our work and mission is a project that the Ascended Masters have asked us to put together on behalf of light-workers and people around the globe. It is called the "Interdimensional Prayer Altar Program"! The Masters have guided us to set this up in the Academy in Agoura Hills, California on the property that we live on. We have set up a "Physical Interdimensional Prayer Altar" where people can send in their prayers on any subject and we will place them on this Altar. In consultation with the Masters, Archangels and Angels, Elohim Masters, and Christed Extraterrestrials, we have set up an arrangement with them that they will immediately work upon all physical letters placed upon this Altar. We have been guided by the inner plane Ascended Masters to create 15 Prayer Altar Programs in different areas of life that people can sign up for. For example, there is one for health and one for financial help in your Spiritual mission. Two-thirds of these programs are totally free. There are five or six that are more advanced Spiritual acceleration programs where written material is sent to you to work with in conjunction with these programs so as to accelerate your Spiritual growth. All letters we receive by e-mail, fax, or letter are placed on the Altar by myself or my personal assistant. It is kept 100% confidential and is an extremely special service provided by the inner plane Ascended Masters and Angels to help all lightworkers and people on Earth with immediate help for whatever they need, should they desire assistance. Other examples of Prayer Altars are: Building your Higher Light Body, Extra Protection, Relationship Help, World Service Prayers, Help for your Animals, Prayer Altar for the Children, Integrating the Goddess, Integrating your Archetypes, Integrating the Seven Rays and working with the Seven Inner Plane Ashrams of the Christ, Integrating the Mantle of the Christ, Ascension Seat Integration, and Light, Love, and Power Body Building Program! These Prayer Altar Programs have been co-created with the inner plane Ascended Masters as another tool for not only helping all lightworkers with whatever they need help with, but also as another cutting-edge tool to accelerate Spiritual evolution!

In a similar regard, the Masters have guided us to set up a Melchizedek Synthesis Light Academy Membership Program which is based on three levels of involvement. Stage One, Stage Two, and Stage Three! Stage One and Stage Three are totally free. Stage Two costs only $20 for a Lifetime Membership with no other fees required. You also receive free large colored pictures of Melchizedek, the Mahatma, Archangel Metatron, and Djwhal Khul for joining. It is not necessary to join to get involved in the work; however, it has been set up by the inner plane Ascended Masters as another service and tool of the Academy to help lightworkers accelerate their Spiritual evolution! When joining the different Stages, the Masters take you under their wing, so to speak, and accelerate your evolution by working with you much more closely on the inner plane while you sleep at night and during your conscious waking hours. The joining is nothing more than a process that gives them the permission to work with you in this more intensive fashion! Again, it is not necessary to join to get involved in the work, and is really just another one of the many fantastic tools and services the Academy has made available to you to accelerate your Spiritual, psychological, and earthly/physical evolution in an integrated and balanced manner!

I had a dream shortly after completing my two new books, *The Golden Book of Melchizedek: How to Become an Integrated Christ/Buddha in This Lifetime*, and my book *How to Release Fear-Based Thinking and Feeling: An In-depth Study of Spiritual Psychology*. In the dream, I was being shown the different Spiritual missions people had. My Spiritual mission was the embodiment of the Holy Spirit. I clearly was shown how other people within GOD, Christ, and the Holy Spirit had missions of being more detached off-shoots of the Holy Spirit, and continuing outward from there, had all kinds of different Spiritual missions. However, mine was the embodiment of the Holy Spirit on Earth.

My Beloved Readers, I want to be very clear here that in sharing this I am in no way, shape, or form claiming to be the Holy Spirit. There is enough glamour in the New Age Movement and I am not interested in adding any more to it. What I am sharing here, which is being given to more clearly and precisely share my Spiritual mission and purpose, is that which I am here to strive to embody and demonstrate. The Holy Spirit is the third aspect of the Trinity of GOD. I have always greatly loved the Holy Spirit, for the Holy Spirit is like the "Voice of GOD"! It is the "Still, Small Voice Within"! When one prays to GOD, the Holy Spirit answers for GOD. The Holy Spirit is the answer to all questions, challenges, and problems. The Holy Spirit speaks for the Atonement or the At-one-ment! It teaches the Sons and Daughters of GOD how to recognize their true identity as God, Christ, the Buddha, and the Eternal Self! In truth, there are only two voices in life! There is the voice of the negative ego and the "Voice of the Holy Spirit"! There is the voice of negative ego/fear-based/separative thinking and feeling, and there is the Voice of God/Spiritual/Christ/Buddha thinking and feeling! There is the "Voice of Love" and the voice of fear! There is the "Voice of Oneness" and the voice of separation!

I was given this dream after completing these two books because, I humbly suggest, this is the energy I was embodying in writing them and that I am striving to embody at all times in my Spiritual mission and purpose on Earth. This is not surprising in the sense that this has always been my Spiritual ideal and the dream was just an inward confirmation in that moment that I was embodying and demonstrating that Spiritual Ideal in the energy flow I was in. This is what I strive to do in all my work, be it my Ascension Book Series, Wesak Celebrations, Teaching, Counseling, Videotapes, Audiotapes, and all my work, which is to strive to be the embodiment of a "Voice for God"! By the grace of GOD, Christ, the Holy Spirit, and the Masters, I provide a lot of the "answers" people and lightworkers are seeking! I teach people how to "undo" negative ego/fear-based/separative thinking and feeling, and show then how to fully realize God/Christ/Buddha thinking and feeling! I show them how to release and undo glamour, illusion, and maya, and instead seek "Truth, as GOD, Christ, the Holy Spirit, and the Masters would have you seek it!"

My real purpose, however, is not to just be the embodiment of the Holy Spirit on Earth, for I would not be embodying the Voice and Vision of the Holy Spirit if I just focused on this. The Voice and Vision of GOD, Christ, the Holy Spirit, and Melchizedek is that of synthesis! This is the other thing I feel in the deepest part of my heart and soul that I am here to embody! So my "truest and highest Spiritual ideal" that I am here to strive to embody, is GOD, Christ, the Holy Spirit, the inner plane Ascended Masters, the Archangels and Angels of the Light of GOD, the Elohim Councils of the Light of GOD, and the Christed Extraterrestrials of the Light of GOD. I feel in the deepest part of my heart and soul, and what I try to embody every moment of my life is "All that is of GOD and the Godforce on Earth!" In this regard, it is my Spiritual mission and purpose to strive to be the embodiment of the "synthesis nature of God on Earth"! This is why I have been given Spiritual leadership of the Synthesis Ashram and Academy on Earth and future leadership of the inner plane Synthesis Ashram that governs our planet.

The Masters also told me that I had achieved my Ascension in the fullest sense of the term and that I did not need to physically die anymore!

I have also been living on Light the last four years; however, this is not something I would recommend everyone do, for the Masters have told me they would actually prefer that almost all lightworkers live on what they call a partial light diet, which is a good healthy physical diet, and also absorb as well. Because of certain factors that are connected with my particular Spiritual Mission and purpose, living on Light has been appropriate for the Spiritual Mission, Spiritual blueprint, puzzle piece, Spiritual contract and Service mission that I came to fulfill!

The other thing I strive to do in my Spiritual mission is to embody Spiritual mastery on a Spiritual, psychological, and physical/earthly level. What most people and lightworkers do not realize is that there are three distinct levels to God Realization. There is a Spiritual level, a psychological level, and a physical/earthly level! To achieve true God Realization, all three levels must be equally mastered! Another way of saying this is that there are "Four Faces of GOD"! There is a Spiritual Face, a Mental Face, an Emotional Face, and a Material Face! To truly realize God, all four must be equally mastered, loved, honored, sanctified, integrated, and balanced! The "Mental and Emotional Faces of GOD" make up the psychological level of GOD. So, my Spiritual mission and purpose is to fully embody Spiritual mastery and unconditional love on all three of these levels and in all Four Faces of GOD! In a similar vein, my Spiritual mission and purpose is to embody self-mastery and proper integration of all "Seven Rays of GOD," not just one or a few. For the "Seven Rays of GOD" are, in truth, the true "Personality of GOD"! My Spiritual mission and purpose is to not only strive to embody all levels of GOD, but to also try and develop all my God-given abilities and Spiritual gifts, on a Spiritual, Psychological, and Physical/Earthly level, and in all Four Faces of GOD!

My Beloved Readers, all these things that I have written about in this chapter are what I strive to fully embody and demonstrate on the Earth every moment of my life, and is what I strive with all my heart and soul and mind and might to teach others to do as well!

As the Founder and Director of the Melchizedek Synthesis Light Academy along with Wistancia, with great humbleness and humility, it has been my great honor and privilege to share "my Spiritual mission and purpose" in a deeper and more profound manner at this time. I do so in the hopes that all who feel a resonance and attunement with this work will get involved with the Academy's "Teachings" and all that it has to offer. I also share this so that all who choose to get involved might join this vast group of lightworkers around the globe, to help spread the teachings and work of the inner plane Ascended Masters. The inner plane Ascended Masters and I, along with the Archangels and Angels, Elohim Councils, and Christed Extraterrestrials, put forth the Clarion

Call to lightworkers around the world to first explore this work, then integrate this work, and then become Ambassadors of the Ascended Masters so we may at this time in Beloved Earth's history bring in fully now the Seventh Golden Age in all its Glory!

About the Author

Dr. Joshua David Stone has a Ph.D. in Transpersonal Psychology and is a licensed Marriage, Family and Child Counselor, in Agoura Hills, California. On a Spiritual level he anchors *The Melchizedek Synthesis Light Academy and Ashram*, which is an integrated inner and outer plane ashram that seeks to represent all paths to God! He serves as one of the leading spokespersons for the Planetary Ascension Movement. Through his books, tapes, workshops, lectures, and annual Wesak Celebrations, Dr. Stone is known as one of the leading Spiritual Teachers and Channels in the world on the teachings of the Ascended Masters, Spiritual Psychology, and Ascension! He has currently written over 31 volumes in his Ascension Book Series, which he also likes to call "The Easy to Read Encyclopedia of the Spiritual Path"!

For a free information packet of all Dr. Stone's workshops, books, audiotapes, Academy membership program, and global outreach program, please call or write to the following address:

Dr. Joshua David Stone
Melchizedek Synthesis Light Academy
28951 Malibu Rancho Rd.
Agoura Hills, CA 91301

Phone: 818-706-8458
Fax: 818-706-8540
e-mail: drstone@best.com

Please come visit my Website at:
http://www.drjoshuadavidstone.com